CARPETS FROM ISLAMIC LANDS

CARPETS FROM ISLAMIC LANDS

FRIEDRICH SPUHLER

Dar al-Athar al-Islamiyyah   The al-Sabah Collection, Kuwait

Copyright © 2012 Gulf Museum Consultancy, WLL, Kuwait
Text copyright © 2012 Friedrich Spuhler

Collection series editor
Salam Kaoukji

Photography and photo-editing
Muhammad Ali

Assisted by
Robert Lorenzo
Michael Tejero

Design by Maggi Smith

First published in 2012 in hardcover in the United States of America by
Thames & Hudson Inc., 500 Fifth Avenue, New York, New York 10110

thamesandhudsonusa.com

Library of Congress Catalog Card Number 2012933046
ISBN 978-0-500-97033-1

Printed and bound in China by C & C Offset Printing Co., Ltd

On the jacket: Detail, Cat. 20 (LNS 27 R)

CONTENTS

PREFACE

by Sheikh Nasser Sabah al-Ahmad al-Sabah

I began to discover my love of historical art during my schooling in Jerusalem in the 1960s. I was particularly enthralled by the monuments of that ancient city, especially her Islamic monuments, which number in the scores and span the seventh to the twentieth centuries AD. As part of my own heritage, these filled me with pride and planted the germ of curiosity about the extent of Islamic artistic achievements.

Such awakened consciousness found expression at the inception of my collecting of Islamic art objects in the mid-1970s. From the beginning, I had an urge to share my enthusiasms for these thrilling remains of the past, an urge also shared by my wife and eventual director of our museum, Sheikha Hussah Sabah al-Salem al-Sabah. Our efforts culminated in the installation of this collection in its own building of the Kuwait National Museum Complex, opened in February 1983, where it was housed and exhibited up to the Iraqi invasion in 1990. The collection was and is of a broad and comprehensive nature, and has continued to be augmented over the years up to the present.

Of all Islamic objects, carpets are surely the most widely known and appreciated. They are also one of the most central types of objects to the daily lives of the people of the time, and by the Middle Ages were in demand in non-Islamic lands. They were the finest carpets in the world, and were treasured in Europe, as shown by their representations in paintings and surviving princely inventories, as well as their physical survival in church treasuries and princely collections.

We have striven to form a collection that is truly representative and of the highest quality possible; and seeing the carpets brought together, presented, described and interpreted by Dr Friedrich Spuhler in this catalogue is a source of enormous satisfaction.

The pleasure and excitement of my first meeting with practically every one of the pieces come back to mind on perusal of this volume, and there are often, as well, memories of the processes by which we were able to give them a good home with worthy companions.

Everyone will have his or her favourites, and some of these are among the finest and most important carpets known, particularly the representatives of great Islamic "classical" types of carpets. But I often find as well that I derive very great gratification from pieces which were probably not courtly but which nevertheless constitute extremely rare and important testimony to the continuity of the carpet-making tradition from the pre-Islamic period. One takes great delight in the phenomenon in which the mind is stimulated when a mere fragment seems to form an intimate window not only to the form and the nature of the decoration of the piece from which it comes, but also to an entire cultural horizon.

It seems fair to say that in historical Islamic culture, even more than most, it is difficult to place the portable objects of utility aside from the "fine" arts, since perhaps the world's most sophisticated decorative traditions find expression here, there and everywhere, and in none of the "crafts" is this more striking than in carpets.

In the end, however, it is the *art* of Islamic and pre-Islamic carpets which has attracted me and driven me to explore its dimensions. Acquisition of the best of these works of art by collections which are made available to scholars and the public prevents their loss or their existence in obscurity, and allows others who are interested to study them. I am confident that making them public in this way, through publications and exhibitions, will result in as yet unimagined insights for many scholars, students and connoisseurs, and provide stimulation of unknown dimensions for a wide range of people around the world. Such, it seems to me, is an appropriate memorial and heritage for the mostly anonymous artists who will thus have managed, in the pursuit of their profession and livelihood, to bequeath such delight and joy to so many.

ACKNOWLEDGMENTS

I shall never forget the moment when I was accompanying Sheikh Nasser al-Sabah around the Museum für Islamische Kunst in Berlin, and he suddenly asked me if I would be willing to write the catalogue of his carpet collection. So to him and to Sheikha Hussah al-Sabah go my profound thanks for initiating this collaboration, and for their personal encouragement throughout this assignment.

Although I was already familiar with the al-Sabah Collection through various publications, at the time I was hardly aware of what my relatively instant acceptance to take on the project was letting me in for. However, I have never had the slightest regret at having agreed to do it. This is due not least to the atmosphere created by the collection's staff in Kuwait, whose friendliness and enthusiasm are beyond anything that I have experienced during my forty years of work with museums. And so my thanks also go to the Dar al-Athar al-Islamiyyah as an institution, and if this may seem a little impersonal, it should not be taken as a sign of lack of consideration. Each of these ever-helpful colleagues created an ambience in which work became a pleasure.

Over five years ago, it was rare to have access to every single item in a collection just by glancing at a database; Salam (Sue) Kaoukji and Manuel Keene, the dynamic duo who drive this team, and who created the collection's database, were always supportive and ready to share their intimate knowledge of the collection, and without Sue's help the not infrequent hiatuses in the work would have gone on far longer. Aurora Luis and Juanna Fernandes never failed to find a solution, no matter what the problem, and Benjamin Hilario and Honorio (Rally) Lim were always at hand to supply me with the required object, no matter how complicated. From the photography department, Muhammed Ali and Robert Lorenzo did admirable work, as did the reliable department of conservation headed by Sophie Budden, assisted by Ahmad al-Enezi. My thanks also go to Deborah Freeman, who was helpful in many ways, and to Layla al-Mussawi, for assisting me in computer-related matters, as well as to Katie Marsh for the painstaking way in which she dealt with matters related to coordination which were essential to the evolution of the project. May this wonderfully cooperative team long remain together, to assist scholars in many more projects.

I would once again like to thank Sheikha Hussah and Sheikh Nasser al-Sabah for creating such an infrastructure and facilitating scholarly work of this kind, so far unique, and for collecting the incredible masterpieces they have assembled in Kuwait.

The work was also made substantially easier through the assistance of my colleagues Anna Jerusalimskaja and Anatol Ivanov in St Petersburg, and Volkmar Enderlein, Claus-Peter Haase and Jens Kröger in Berlin.

This manuscript could never have been put together without the massive input from my wife Julia Plato, whose computer skills, drafting diagrams, identification of textile structures and trained eye spotted so many things that I had missed. She contributed more than her fair share both to the research in Kuwait and to the writing of this book.

Friedrich Spuhler

THE 2,500-YEAR HISTORY OF ORIENTAL CARPETS

Until 1949, when Sergei I. Rudenko discovered the Pazyryk carpet in a Scythian burial mound in the Altai Mountain range of southern Siberia,[1] the history of oriental carpets derived, to a large extent, from examples found in the treasuries of churches, and the treasuries and palaces of emperors and kings, as well as in the stately homes of the nobility who had had contacts with the East, resulting either from trade or from war.

With the Pazyryk carpet now dated from the fifth to fourth century BC, we are faced with the unprecedented instance of an excavated carpet preserved in its original size. Moreover, its state of preservation differs substantially from that of other finds, because pile and colours often survive better under the protection of earth or ice.

It is likewise noteworthy that the earliest pile carpets exhibit borders around their edges, and that their central fields are either decorated with large figural motifs or are divided into compartments with smaller repetitive motifs. The concept of the central medallion is a much later development.

There is a gap of almost 1,700 years between the example from Pazyryk and the earliest Seljuq carpets from Anatolia of the thirteenth century. However, the pre-Islamic carpet fragments from the al-Sabah Collection, details of which are presented here for the first time, reduce this gap to around 600 years, providing us with examples from the second to the sixth century, following which there is a break that lasts until the thirteenth century, but this is no longer considered a major gap.

Thanks to recent Sasanian finds, the original 1,700-year gap can now be divided into three roughly equal periods of around 600 years each. The first, which extends from the period of the Pazyryk carpet to that of the earliest Sasanian pile carpets, covers six centuries for which virtually no examples exist. The new Sasanian-era finds from Afghanistan that are represented here originate from various stages of the second period, and a complete overview and publication about this part of the collection will ensue once conservation of the carpet fragments has been completed. Following a brief examination of the pre-Islamic group of fragments, the third and classical period will be discussed here, with references to a selection of types from other collections.

PART I
PRE-CLASSICAL CARPETS

CHAPTER ONE
PRE-ISLAMIC AND EARLY ISLAMIC CARPETS

CARPETS FROM THE SASANIAN PERIOD[1]

At present, only a few fragments of pile carpets from the Sasanian period (AD 224–651) have been published, and information about such examples has been so scattered that it has not been possible to establish an evolutionary history of the type as an independent group. Thanks to Sheikh Nasser Sabah al-Ahmad al-Sabah's remarkable devotion both to collecting and to conservation, a substantial gap in the early history of pile carpets has now been filled, and these uncharted Sasanian examples can now be studied, albeit in the form of fragments, and will hopefully serve to provide a few answers to some intriguing issues. Fortunately, the original dimensions of two examples in the collection can be determined, and this constitutes a sensational development. In total there are around two dozen fragments from findspots in north-eastern Afghanistan which reportedly originated from burial grounds in the province of Samangan, particularly from the cave of Ayr Malik in the village of Duab-i Shahpasand. The reliability of dealers' information remains open to question, but the recurrence of the name Samangan over the years means that it certainly cannot be excluded as a genuine findspot. Indeed, there is no reason why these carpets could not have originated in this province of present-day Afghanistan, since during the Sasanian period it was part and parcel of the great Persian Empire, and remained so through to the reign of the Timurids (AH 771–913/AD 1370–1507).

The colours and coarse texture of the pre-Islamic carpet fragments in the al-Sabah Collection are not sufficiently distinctive to permit a division into groups, but carbon-14 dating of the material has allowed the finds to be divided into three groups, with the earliest fragments dating from the turn of the second century to the early Sasanian period. The first example we will consider here is a detail from a carpet of the compartmented type, datable to AD 240–280, that features a striding stag with its head lowered, causing the typical horizontally oriented antlers to be depicted vertically (Fig. 3).[2] The fragment (Fig. 4),[3] from a slightly earlier period,

Fig. 3: detail, carpet fragment LNS 47 R a

Fig. 4: detail, carpet fragment LNS 64 R

is comprised of part of a plain dark brown field, an inner wave pattern stripe, and an unusual and lively outer guard or main border composed of two rows of rectangles of alternating colours, each of which is subdivided into a diagonally arranged *ton-sur-ton* chequered pattern.

An intermediary group, datable to around AD 240–540, which constitutes the start of the peak period of Sasanian art, is represented here by the detail of a fragment showing a winged mythical creature with curly mane in a field defined by a minor wave border and a main border of counterchanging leaf motifs (Fig. 5).[4] The other two fragment details (Fig. 6 and Fig. 7), datable from around AD 310 to 370, are from the edges of a rug with a relatively wide border likewise comprised of a minor wave pattern and counterchanging leaf motifs. Interestingly, the large paws of a feline encroach on the wave pattern border of one of the fragments, whereas a pair of stylized tulips in classic Sasanian style is laid out parallel to the border of the other fragment.[5] The slightly bluish tone of the red colour was most probably obtained with cochineal dye, which is what gives this carpet a relatively dark appearance

that is not found in any of the other fragments. The detail of the corner fragment (Fig. 2),[6] in which two foliate scrolls abut on one another, is a good example of how the designer tried to resolve the perpetual problem of corner configuration. The two fragments from "hunting carpets", which bring our prefatory selection of details from the pre-Islamic fragment collection to a close, both feature stags which are probably part of a procession of deer from a royal hunt. They are represented with elaborate antlers and hold their heads high facing right. The stag depicted in Fig. 8[7] appears to hold a blossom in its snout, while the other wears a fluttering filet in typical Sasanian style (Fig. 9).[8] The datable flatweave (Fig. 10), meanwhile, can be placed shortly towards the end of the Sasanian era.[9]

All the examples are of unusually thick and stiff structure which is partly, but not entirely, due to residual dirt from conditions of burial underground. Wool is always used for the warp, weft and pile, the yarn is bulky and crudely spun, and they are woven in the asymmetric knot that matches the method applied to all carpets originating from Iran and further east. Cruder knots are discernible on the reverse of the fragments (roughly every three to five rows), and incorporate a rather arbitrary range of materials that include pieces of unspun wool along with strips of cloth and leather of differing widths, as well as the woollen yarn used for the face. The thickness of the carpets must have served for insulation, and it is likely that they served as floor covers in tents. The longest carpet that can be reconstructed measures around 2.5 metres in length, and some examples are up to 1.5 metres wide. The direction of the pile is naturally always vertical, as when horizontal weaves became commonplace it resulted in a pile that ran counter to the pattern. Stylistically, the animal motifs are arranged in some sort of procession or individually within compartments. Centralized designs, for example ones using medallions, did not feature during this period, but borders both with and without guard stripes were already commonplace. The processions of quadrupeds and compartmentalized layouts recall the design of the Pazyryk carpet, but there is not the slightest structural resemblance between them. The fine knots of the Pazyryk carpet are regular and symmetrical, which suggests a long tradition of carpet weaving, whereas the knots of these examples are quite crude. The vivid colours are comprised of primary blue, red and yellow together with shades thereof, light blue, sandalwood red (*santalum album*), pink, bright yellow, as well as two shades of green. Undyed wool was used for the various shades of white, brown and black.

Fig. 5: detail, carpet fragment LNS 74 R

Fig. 6: detail, carpet fragment LNS 67 R d

Fig. 7: detail, carpet fragment LNS 67 R b

If one takes into account the description of the "Spring of Khosrau" carpet, which was allegedly found in the palace of the Sasanian ruler Khosrau I at Ctesiphon in AD 637, and embroidered with gemstones and pearls,[10] it is clear that the pile carpets presented here were anything but luxury goods for courtly use. Both stylistically and in terms of execution they would have been suitable for use as tent-floor covers, and would likely also have served as bedding and as insulation to ward off the cold of the ground. Furthermore, looms of up to 1.5 metres in width would have fitted in with the requirements of the nomadic way of life.

THE EARLY ISLAMIC PRE-CLASSICAL PERIOD

The course of oriental carpet history after the Sasanian period, or from the start of the Islamic era in the seventh century until the thirteenth century, is almost impossible to trace because of the paucity of surviving examples. Carpets from central Anatolia dating from the end of this "vacant" period were discovered in mosques at Konya and in neighbouring Beyshehir, but the scattered examples from this period available for study unfortunately do not form a group characteristic of a particular dynasty, such as we shall see in our discussion on classical carpets. Furthermore, a technique is also at issue, as these are not pile carpets in the strictest sense of the term, that is carpets in which knots were tied in horizontal rows and then cut. This particular group of early "pile rugs" were executed using the looped pile method rather than knots, wherein the yarn was threaded around a wooden rod laid across the surface, and when each row of loops was completed the loops were slit in half thus releasing the rod. This cut-loop or cut-pile technique was particularly popular in the eastern regions of the Mediterranean, and examples survive from Fustat and Akhmim in Upper Egypt. One such example is in the Keir Collection, London, and is comprised of fairly large fragments,[11] yet its Byzantine, predominantly geometric, pattern of rectangles, squares and octagons seems to have had little influence on pile carpet design after the turn of the first millennium (a proposed reconstruction of the Keir Collection carpet was published by Gantzhorn).[12] At most, this pattern may have had some influence on the so-called Mamluk carpets of Egypt,[13] but only if one were to discount the alternative suggestion that both patterns developed from Eastern Mediterranean floor mosaics, such as those from the Umayyad palace of Khirbat al-Mafjar (724–43).[14] It must, however, be kept in mind that in eastern Iran, where our Sasanian fragments come from, asymmetrical knots had long been in use.

We shall discuss the early development of the classical carpet, that is the period from the eleventh century onward, in the chapters on Turkey and Persia, which consequently allows us to say that there is no considerable gap in the history of oriental carpets despite the fact that the al-Sabah Collection does not include examples representative of the medieval Islamic period.

Surveys of Islamic art tend to study individual art forms, such as carpets and textiles, ceramics or metalwork, within a dynastic context guided by its architecture which in turn was generally steered by the taste of individual rulers. In fact the decorative arts were far more dependent on technical and stylistic traditions, and were consequently less closely connected to the changes in dynastic styles. In other words, the decorative arts were more subject to individual processes of change, as the work was not as closely bound to the taste of current rulers as was architecture, therefore inconsistencies in style should more likely be attributed to regional and traditional departures from mainstream production. Good examples of this are the so-called "Holbein" and "Lotto" carpets (see Chapter 3), which were unquestionably produced during the Ottoman period, but which have little or nothing in common with what is generally

Fig. 8: detail, carpet fragment LNS 71 R

Fig. 9: detail, carpet fragment LNS 62 R a

by the upper merchant classes and guilds. These high-status examples have long constituted the sole foundations on which our historical framework for evaluating carpets is constructed. But the reality of pile carpet production does not reflect this discriminatory selection. Rural carpets and examples produced for personal use must have existed in far greater quantities, even if they were not deemed suitable for export. Indeed, they were virtually unknown in European collections and only a few scattered examples made their way into the collections of Berlin's museums in the late nineteenth century, and until late into the second half of the twentieth century were the subject of wildly inaccurate assessments.

Since pile carpets and flatweaves were essential items in all rural households and nomadic tents, and were moreover part of a tradition altogether distinct from that of workshop production, one could comfortably say that carpets were simultaneously produced for three different social levels of society, with varying standards of style and motifs. Rural carpets did not include cotton, which was the workshop's preferred material for warp and weft, and obviously silk was completely out of the question. The sheen of wool was naturally vibrant, but because these carpets were subjected to extensive use they eventually faded and wore out, and very few examples remain from between the fifteenth and eighteenth centuries. The only opportunity to see and study them – as Balpınar and Hirsch were able to do[15] – was in mosques, which had acquired them as *waqf* (charitable endowments).

It was not until the eighteenth and nineteenth centuries that a more comprehensive documentation became available, because this is when, in addition to urban workshop productions, rural and tribal carpets were exported to Europe and America. Most of our knowledge of carpets from this period is based on the experience of traders who travelled to the East in search of goods.

The relationship between carpets and other fields of Islamic art was by no means the only way to secure accurate information regarding their attribution; another unique approach to documentation was obtained through the representation of oriental carpets in European paintings. As many painters were attracted by the resplendent colours and exotic patterns of oriental carpets this led to an extensive corpus of *terminus ante quem* date attributions, and these paintings constituted a vast repertoire of examples whose individual histories served to date them more or less accurately. Following this come the special commissions and gifts, most of which

known as the Ottoman court style, their roots lying far closer to Timurid and Seljuq art. Insistence on linking artefacts with dynasties inevitably leads to inaccurate attributions, unless the timeframe is treated with flexibility. This goes some way to explain the problem that resulted from the categorization of carpets on the basis of pattern type and country of origin that was so widespread around one hundred years ago, and led to a free-standing view of the history of oriental carpets which lost sight of the history of Islamic art as a whole. The approach resulted in a flood of books on oriental carpets that did not fulfil the demands of true scholarship, and often failed to reach the standards required of a simple handbook. In no other field have there been as many amateur publications as in that of oriental carpets.

In the scholarly literature on classical oriental carpets, the "yardsticks of consequence" have traditionally been courtly examples belonging to church treasuries or acquired for royal coronations and weddings, as well as those used as table covers were well documented, as well as the exceptional cases in which coats of arms were incorporated in the design in a typically European manner. Dated carpets – four such examples have been authenticated[16] – are one-off specimens, which means that they are of limited usefulness for dating other carpets.

In around the fifteenth century, the keen interest taken by Europeans in the lives of the people of the East led to extensive travel which resulted in a number of travel accounts. Every diplomatic mission and trading expedition produced some kind of published narrative. The splendour of the Eastern courts was intoxicating, and carpets were among the most esteemed luxury goods although descriptions of them were usually cursory. It is only when their gold and silver threads elicited particular admiration that more precise details were recorded.[17]

Thanks to the comparatively recent technique of carbon-14 dating, it is now possible to determine the true age of materials. Although this method was originally used to detect forgeries, it is now carried out to determine dates, thus contributing to the precise attribution of various examples from the rich corpus of Anatolian kilims and Turkmen pile carpets.

As the al-Sabah Collection holds an extensive range of classical carpets, it makes sense to classify them according to dynasties, which incorporates both date and geographical origin. Only one example of peasant pile carpets is included in the collection (Cat. 10), which is regrettable since a large number of such pieces have become available since the 1990s.

Fig. 10: detail, textile fragment LNS 1085 T

PART II
CLASSICAL CARPETS

CHAPTER TWO
EGYPT

MAMLUK CARPETS

During the Mamluk period (AH 648–922/AD 1250–1517), especially in the second half of the fifteenth and early sixteenth centuries, a very distinctive type of carpet was produced in Egypt for use at court as well as for export to Europe. Fortunately, the exhaustive and definitive study by Kurt Erdmann, "Kairener Teppiche, Teil 1: Europäische und islamische Quellen des 15.–18. Jahrhunderts", brought together a number of European and Islamic sources which leave no doubt that the centre of production was Cairo.[1] Furthermore, the stylistic features of these rugs are so in keeping with other Mamluk decorative arts such as metalwork,[2] woodwork,[3] Qur'an manuscripts[4] and bookbindings[5] that this attribution was never questioned in over a century of art-historical research.

The field designs of Mamluk carpets are all characterized by polygonal shapes and stars, stylized plant motifs including cypress trees, palms and papyrus plants, always arranged in a linear or centralized configuration, generally with borders comprised of rosettes alternating with cartouches. The style is remarkably uniform, thus scarcely no propensity for a different dating exists; consequently the entire production of the type cannot have lasted more than half a century. Furthermore, it can be inferred that there was a single place of production or central workshop making carpets both for export, mainly to Venice,[6] and for the Mamluk court. And whereas only a few large-format Mamluk carpets of courtly style are known, including one with a silk pile which is among the most beautiful carpets in the world,[7] thanks to this example and to another that was not discovered until 1982 – a wool-pile Mamluk carpet almost 11 metres long that belonged to the Medicis[8] – there can no longer be any doubt concerning the existence of workshops attached to the court. Another characteristic worthy of note is the existence among Mamluk carpets of two predominant sizes: the small-format Mamluk carpets that are around 200 cm long and 140 cm wide, give or take 5 to 10 per cent, which represent approximately 70 per cent of extant examples; and the large-format Mamluk carpets that measure 400 cm by 200 cm, once again with variables of around 5 to 10 per cent which account for another 15 per cent of extant carpets. The remainder is made up of carpets of unusual dimensions and forms, including square and circular examples.

The central axis of these carpets is generally comprised of either a single or a line-up of three or five octagonal or star-shaped medallions with patterns comparable to ones seen through a kaleidoscope, a seemly image that Wilhelm von Bode was the first to use. The polygonal stars and centralized layout likewise share design similarities with Mamluk woodwork, bookbindings and metalwork, as well as with book illumination and floor mosaics, as was pertinently suggested by Friedrich Sarre[9] and Edmund de Unger.[10]

The utilization of soft and lustrous wool serves to intensify the fascinating interplay of colours, which generally consist of cherry red, pale blue and light green, as well as the occasional use of yellow and additional shades of blue, although the last two are very rare. And, as is the case with Safavid court carpet-weaving structures, they are woven with asymmetrical knots and only use S-spun wool, two characteristic elements of the Cairo workshops which later take on a determining role when the need to pinpoint the origin of some of the carpets commissioned by the Ottomans in Cairo arises. In earlier literature, this group was often classified as "Damascus carpets", a matter of long-winded dispute among scholars that lasted until 1921, when Friedrich Sarre made a convincing case for Cairo, which Erdmann corroborated in his detailed account of 1938.[11]

Cat. 1 MAMLUK CARPET
Cairo, circa 1500

Length: 378 cm, width 220 cm
Warp: wool, yellowish, S4Z
Weft: wool, shades of red, S2–3Z, 3 shoots
Knots: wool, S2–3, asymmetrical, V 39, H 35
Selvedge: 4–6 threads, overcast in red
Ends: approx. 1 cm light blue kilim
Provenance: art market, 1970s–80s
Literature: Jenkins, Keene and Bates 1983, p. 103;
Denny 1999, p. 9

Inv. no. LNS 14 R

Detail, Cat. 1 (LNS 14 R)

Detail, Cat. 1 (LNS 14 R)

The uniformity of Mamluk carpet designs has already been discussed in the introduction to this section; however, closer inspection serves to reveal differences in quality, especially with respect to the combination of motifs and the corresponding uses of colour. When the colour palette is limited to three colours, the determining factor becomes the expanse and position allocated to a particular colour in the design.

Why is this Mamluk carpet considered the more "glamorous" of the two examples in the al-Sabah Collection? For a start, one should consider the contrasting colours of the predominantly green medallions on either side of the central octagon, which, although likewise predominantly green, is skilfully augmented with red. Projecting from the central octagon are green linear and pointed "rays" on a red ground, the contrast of which gives off an impression of chatoyance that further serves to draw attention to the central octagon. Ultimately, the pattern serves to draw one's attention to the central eight-pointed star executed in shades of yellow positioned at the intersection of the long and short axes, which offsets the design and emphasizes the glowing effect. Comparisons to a jewel in its setting would not be inappropriate.

There are few instances in which the border complements the field as beautifully and harmoniously as in this example. This is accomplished by the intricate interweaving of the red umbrella-like papyrus plant motifs on the green ground, which makes very effective use of *abrash* (or the effect produced by the uneven tones of different lots of dyed yarn). The same colour combination recurs in reverse, green and blue on a red ground, in rectangular panels in the four corners of the main field. The blend of single and dual colour surfaces serves to supplement the overall harmony of the design, and its unusual fine state of preservation allows the impact of these colouristic effects to successfully stand out.

The format of this carpet merits a final comment. Another Mamluk carpet of roughly the same size was recorded in 1615 in the inventory of the Fugger family[12] (merchants from Augsburg in Bavaria), and is known to have been used as a table covering. In the East, the use of carpets as table coverings would have been out of the question, but in Europe it was deemed acceptable because it served to protect exotic collectibles from wear and tear, as well as to show off their beauty to full and dignified effect. The more common small-format Mamluk carpets were used to cover altar-steps, another practice that allowed them to be displayed in a manner befitting their status.

Cat. 2 MAMLUK CARPET
Cairo, circa 1500

Length: 442 cm, width 267 cm
Warp: wool, greenish blue, S3Z
Weft: wool, white and yellowish, S2Z,
2 shoots
Knots: wool, S2–3, asymmetrical, V 40, H 40
Selvedge: not original
Ends: not original
Provenance: art market, 1977
Literature: Denny 1999, p. 11;
Curatola 2010, cat. 104

Inv. no. LNS 13 R

Although this is a large-format rug, it displays features that are typical of the small-format Mamluk carpets. The design centres on a large motif that occupies the full width of the field, which is flanked at the top and bottom by two horizontal bands of equal width. Both bands consist of three octagons, each set within an octagonal border of star-burst motifs alternating with eight-pointed stars, and serve to offset the inner field from the narrow end borders.

Projecting from the edges of the central octagonal star are four rectangles formed by the extension of the structural lines of the star, which intersects the inner guard border, setting off a square field. This configuration allowed the central star medallion to expand beyond its regular outline and fill the entire field of the carpet, thus extending over 2 metres. This type of field division matches that of smaller-format Mamluk carpets, although the horizontal bands would generally have been decorated with rows of palms and cypresses, and the ratio of length to width would have been 1:1.2. Therefore, although this second Mamluk carpet from the al-Sabah Collection is quite large, its design nevertheless reflects that of the small-format variety, which leads one to think that this exceptional piece may have been a special commission.

The distribution of reds and greens is strikingly uniform, creating an overall balanced look, although lacking the contrast and relief effects of the preceding example.

Detail, Cat. 2 (LNS 13 R)

Cat. 3 FRAGMENT OF AN
AUBUSSON CARPET IN
THE MAMLUK STYLE
France, mid-18th century

Length 377 cm, width 351 cm
Warp: wool (?), coarse and light-coloured,
Z5S
Weft: wool (?), light blue, Z;
and wool, white and brown, Z2S
Knots: symmetrical 2–3Z, V 24, H 22–23
Provenance: art market, 1980s
Literature: Denny 1999, p. 13;
Carboni 1999, p. 100

Inv. no. LNS 33 R

Over sixty years ago, the fragment of a carpet with a design and layout in Mamluk style was published in a French book on carpets[13] which should not necessarily be counted as a serious contribution to the literature on the subject. The book might well have been completely forgotten today were it not for the impressive colour plate of the so-called "Damascus carpet", which was preceded by black-and-white illustrations of two small-format Mamluk rugs that the author, obviously unaware of the already extensive literature on Mamluk carpets, designated as "Hispano-Arab". One glance at this unusual fragment was enough to confirm that the provenance could not possibly have been Cairo. So what were we to make of this rather crudely woven "outsider" which was often alluded to in serious publications about Mamluk carpets? Even Charles Grant Ellis, who was always ready to tackle issues relating to the grey areas in our field, mentioned it in conjunction with a larger fragment[14] that is surely related to fragments published by Achdjian, and the example in the al-Sabah Collection, and said that he could not exclude the possibility of it having been produced in North Africa. His wish to remain non-committal was understandable, especially since I assume that Ellis had not seen any of the three above-mentioned examples. When the carpet from the al-Sabah Collection was first exhibited in 1999 at the Islamic Arts Museum Malaysia in Kuala Lumpur, together with some of the important carpets from the collection, the curator of the exhibition retained the label "North Africa" or "Maghreb", and Stefano Carboni reiterated the same attribution in his review of the exhibition.[15]

But the discovery, at an auction of oriental and European carpets, of an example closely related to the three above-mentioned fragments, and whose medallion clearly has its roots in eighteenth-century European carpet designs, provided the answer to the true provenance of this type of rug.[16] Clearly this was a European production, and in all probability the source was Aubusson, where large-format carpets based on oriental models were commissioned by Louis XIV for use at court. In earlier times, fortunes were spent on importing carpets from Turkey and Cairo, but in the period in question even the court cut its costs with replicas woven on local looms.

There are also technical differences that cannot be overlooked. In contrast to similar carpets from Cairo, the knots are symmetrical, and the use of coarse materials for the warp and weft makes the resulting carpet rough to the touch. In her essay on this group of Aubusson carpets, Elisabeth Floret includes another fragment which she dates "circa 1750".[17]

These were not isolated cases. As far back as the sixteenth and seventeenth centuries in England[18] and Spain, "Turkish" carpet designs were copied from the repertoire of "Holbein" and "Lotto" carpets. The principal difference lay in the loss of adequate geometric patterns that characterize the Cairo-made originals: telling details include the uneven contours of the central field, and the carrot-like palm leaves that border the medallion.

CHESSBOARD CARPETS

Chessboard carpets form a homogeneous group of carpets with an easily recognizable field design that is not dissimilar to a chessboard. They feature repeating rows of hexagons, enclosing radially arranged filler motifs of miniature cypress trees and stylized plants, evocative of the decorative elements in Mamluk carpets. Another similarity lies in the consistent colour combination of light blue and bluish-green details together with some white against a light vermilion ground, and it is worthy of note that the hexagons are always the same size, regardless of the format of the carpet. This uniformity has led people into overestimating the number of extant chessboard carpets, when, in fact, just over forty examples are known to be in existence. The number of hexagons varies between six and thirty-five, and at least a third of the small-format carpets feature a two-by-three arrangement of hexagons. These, along with three-quarters of all chessboard carpets, have a typical border of alternating rosettes and elongated cartouches.

The example in the al-Sabah Collection (Cat. 4) is one of a group of large-format carpets with complex and highly varied borders, which can be traced back to carpet designs of the Safavid and Ottoman type. Here the distinction between field and border is very clear. In addition, the chessboard carpet workshops made mistakes with the rhythm of the vine meanders as well as in their skewed attempts at resolving the problems of corner compositions. In light of what we have discussed so far, if we were to make an interim appraisal concerning the nature of the ateliers which produced these carpets, it would be that heterogeneous elements of this type would be in keeping with the methods of weavers working on a large number of pieces, and essentially on commission.

An important factor in assessing this group is the treatment of materials. For example, the knots are of the asymmetrical type as is the case in Mamluk carpets; however, by contrast, the wool for the warp, weft and pile is always Z-spun. This corresponds to Turkish carpets, as does the use of red-dyed wool for the weft. Thus the technique is a blend of Turkish and Egyptian methods, and can therefore not be attributed with certainty to either production centre. The origin must therefore lie elsewhere, and there is no shortage of suggestions in the relevant literature: Damascus, Rhodes and the Adana Plain in Turkey. The current favourite is Damascus. If we retain technique as a criterion for the attribution of the group, we should consider other examples which not only present a stylistic dissonance between field and border but in which the whole field has little in common with the original pattern of hexagons. The *Museum* für Islamische Kunst in Berlin includes an outsider to the group,[19] whose field consists of a complex arrangement of "Safavid-Ottoman" cloudbands, and which I have already discussed together with a few comparable examples in an article specifically devoted to chessboard carpets.[20]

Since this group is stylistically singularly varied, we are faced with the question of what kind of workshops might have produced such a variety of styles. It may be that the weavers and designers came from different production centres, and if one were to disregard the possibility of Cairo, the centre could only have been Damascus. Although the city had no weaving tradition prior to that of chessboard carpets, it was a sufficiently large urban centre to produce carpets by commission. The geometric, hexagon-based design may hark back to Mamluk traditions of the first half of the sixteenth century, with Safavid-Ottoman variations – especially in the borders – and may have persisted to the end of that century.

Detail, Cat. 4 (LNS 46 R)

Cat. 4 CHESSBOARD CARPET
Damascus or Cairo, circa 1600

Length: 291 cm, width 185 cm
Warp: wool, white, Z2S
Weft: wool, pink, Z, 2x, 1st wavy,
2nd straight
Knots: wool, Z2, asymmetrical, V 39,
H 28–29
Former
Collection: van Loo, Rome
Provenance: art market, 1996
Literature: Christie's 1996, lot 417

Inv. no. LNS 46 R

Detail, Cat. 4 (LNS 46 R)

This positively glowing chessboard rug is one of the best examples of this small group. The fifteen identical hexagons, arranged in rows of three by five, enclose interlaced star motifs of octagonal outline rendered in two alternating colour variations: a red hexagon with a blue star interlace on a pale green ground filled with geometrically arranged floral motifs; and in the adjacent hexagon a green star interlace with floral motifs on a pale blue ground. It is precisely this alternation of colour schemes that creates the chessboard effect. Around each individual star interlace are small, identical cypress trees and composite flowers.

The broad blue border with the vine meander, which, as discussed above, is somewhat exceptional for carpets of this type, features pairs of mirrored bifurcated palmettes issuing from lotus blossoms in counterchanging orientation along the vine. Two comparable examples – now in the Vakıflar Museum in Istanbul[21] – come from the Ulu Mosque in Divrigi, eastern Anatolia, which might imply that the inspiration for these unusual borders may have come from eastern Anatolia. We can only hope that the future will lead to finds of further comparable pieces that will bring us closer to a solution regarding their origin, so that following over eighty years of speculation and guesswork the search for their provenance may finally come to an end.

CHAPTER THREE
TURKEY

SELJUQ CARPETS
Our discussion about Turkish carpets will begin with an overview of a group of Turkish pile carpets that are not represented in the al-Sabah Collection, but which nonetheless merit attention since they pre-date the earliest Turkish examples in the collection.[1]

KONYA CARPETS
In 1907, F. R. Martin discovered three large and several small rug fragments in the Alaeddin Mosque at Konya (central Anatolia),[2] the city that gave its name to the type, and was once a capital of the Seljuqs of Rum, the dynasty that ruled Anatolia until AH 707/AD 1307. Together with additional small fragments, plus one that, at the time of its discovery, was still preserved in its original format and came from the Eshrefoglu Mosque at Beyshehir (around 80 kilometres south-west of Konya), these constitute the small group of "Konya" or "Seljuq" carpets. Their thirteenth-century dating matches the completion of the mosque's extension (1218–20) – a plausible reason for their production – although there is no evidence of a connection. They are generally described as small-pattern carpets, in that they have no central medallions, their borders are wide and unsophisticated, and the weaving is crude and not dissimilar to village rugs of a much later date, although compared with later Ushak carpets, the colours are handled with greater subtlety.

The Konya carpets now kept in the Türk ve Islam Eserleri Müzesi in Istanbul have been published often enough in sufficient detail to make further reproduction here unnecessary.

Among the contemporary Seljuq carpets discovered at Beyshehir was a large-format example first published by Rudolf Riefstahl in 1931, but which was hardly ever published in the subsequent literature.[3] Riefstahl's black-and-white photograph showed only one-half of the carpet which, furthermore, since the piece was hung on a line for the purpose of photography, was consequently only partially visible. In the early 1960s, this carpet reappeared in Europe intact, and was offered to what was then the Islamic Department of the Staatliche Museen

zu Berlin, but Kurt Erdmann rejected the offer. The half that was not recorded photographically in Riefstahl's account was published in 1978 by the Keir Collection, London,[4] and, years later, the second half resurfaced in the David Collection in Copenhagen, by way of a London dealer.[5]

ANATOLIAN ANIMAL CARPETS
Following, in chronological order, is the small-pattern group known as the Anatolian animal rugs. Until 1988 there were only two known examples of the type,[6] but with seven additional carpets having since been discovered, this group has undergone the most surprising development.[7] Since the 1990s new examples have emerged from Tibet. During China's Cultural Revolution (1957–65) Tibetan monasteries lost many important works of art, which were either destroyed or, understandably, removed by the banished monks. This was how many Anatolian animal carpets eventually ended up in the safety of museums and private collections. Woven in Turkey during the fourteenth and fifteenth centuries, not a single specimen from this group has survived in its land of origin. Indeed, it is only due to their challenging travels along the Silk Road, and shelter in the monasteries of Tibet, that they have survived at all.

Assigning dates to carpets on the basis of comparable depictions in European paintings was a method adopted at a very early stage in the historiography of the oriental carpet, and was a technique adopted by the researchers known as the "Berlin School". Furthermore, it was a painting by Domenico di Bartolo[8] that allowed Wilhelm von Bode in 1902 to attribute the "dragon and phoenix" carpet, that ended up in Rome in 1886, to the first half of the fifteenth century.

The first example of an Anatolian animal carpet to come from Tibet after the 1980s owes its immediate acquisition by the New York Metropolitan Museum of Art to a painted parallel in an early fifteenth-century work by a Sienese artist.[9] In this carpet, four particularly stylized quadrupeds enclose a similar three-legged animal with a proportionately small head and a curled-up tail. This motif is repeated three times in the painted version, which in addition has a Kufic-style border, whereas the original features a border with rows of octagons whose hooked motif is more in keeping with woven patterns.

The treatment of the animals is almost identical to the ones depicted on the most famous Anatolian animal carpet which was formerly in the Orient Stars Collection.[10] Generally these animal representations are very stylized and are inferior to the Sasanian animal motifs described in Chapter 1. Stylistic connections should therefore not be contemplated in this case; however, shared roots may be found in early Islamic textiles.

OTTOMAN CARPETS
"HOLBEIN" AND "LOTTO" CARPETS
"Umbrella" terminology is common in carpet literature, and there is little point in disputing the usage. The common names used to designate the carpets in this section go back to the earliest days when experts studied carpets by means of their reproductions in European paintings. In 1532 Hans Holbein the Younger painted a portrait of *The Merchant Georg Gisze* (now in the Gemäldegalerie, Berlin), which included a carpet used as a table cover. Its pattern matched that of a group of carpets that since 1902 has consequently been designated as "Holbein carpets". Similar carpets are depicted in paintings dating from the mid-fifteenth century to around 1600, but most surviving examples are fragmentary, with very few pieces preserved in their original size.

The fields of these carpets are mainly comprised of vertical and horizontal rows of essentially square-shaped compartments, straddled at their points of contact or corners by rhomboid motifs of foliate arabesques. The compartments are either presented in a chessboard arrangement of alternating red and dark blue ground, or on a predominantly red monochrome ground. Each compartment encloses an octagon of equal size, in two alternating colours and outlined with eight interlaced knot motifs, while their centres are marked by a star.

Their borders are generally classified into two types: the version found on earlier examples which consists of a repetitive angular interlace of hooked hastae that resemble floriated Kufic

script and are oriented towards the carpet's outer edge; and the later and more common version, which is far less ornate than the older "calligraphic" type, and consists of a continuous angular interlace with identical inner and outer edges. All motifs have contouring lines, and the predominant colours are various shades of red, along with blue, yellow, white and green.

Small-pattern "Holbein" carpets must have been very popular in Europe, just as the so-called "Lotto" carpets were. Much rarer, however, are the large-pattern "Holbein" rugs, which consist of fewer and much larger squares that are always aligned along the longer axis of the rug and clearly separated from one another. The town of Ushak in western Anatolia is regarded as the source of the small-pattern variety, while the large-pattern form is believed to have originated from Bergama in western Turkey. Between the fifteenth and nineteenth centuries, Ushak is thought to have been the production centre for many types of carpets that are often related to each other by colour but rarely by pattern. And perhaps, rather than their usual attribution to Ushak, it might in fact be more suitable to assign them to western Anatolia, as examples reliably associated with Ushak itself are in very short supply.

It is also believed that the so-called "Lotto" carpets were woven in western Anatolia.[11] Lorenzo Lotto, along with other Italian and Dutch masters, used such carpets like theatrical props in his paintings. For example, one is depicted hanging over a parapet in his altarpiece for the Basilica di San Giovanni e Paolo in Venice.[12]

Both the "Holbein" and "Lotto" carpet designs are essentially laid out with rows of octagons and have staggered rows of cruciform motifs in their interstices, but the design of the "Lotto" variety is always featured in yellow accented with blue patches, and with dark contouring lines against a red ground. The "Lotto" borders are only of interest in the early examples, when they correspond to the angular Kufic-like elements of the "Holbein" carpets. The "Lotto" pattern endured until the late eighteenth century, but predominantly only on small-format carpets that tended to have awkwardly crowded fields.

Cat. 5 "HOLBEIN" CARPET
Western Anatolia, circa 1500

Length: 287 cm, width 140 cm (fragment)
Warp: wool, white, Z2S
Weft: wool, red, Z, 2x
Knots: wool, symmetrical, 2Z, V 32, H 34
Provenance: art market, 1980s
Literature: Salmon 1984, p. 177;
Varichon 1989, p. 61;
Carboni 1999, p. 101;
Denny 1999, p. 5

Inv. no. LNS 22 R

Detail, Cat. 5 (LNS 22 R)

This fragmentary "Holbein" carpet is comprised of a fully preserved field of four by seven and a half rows of chequered compartments. These are laid out on alternating red and dark blue ground, echoed by the colour alternation of the red and white central octagons, and have rows of rhomboid arabesque motifs straddling the points of intersection of the compartments. And, although it is unusual for the field to end with a row of halved compartments, I am not inclined to see this as an accident, but rather as the result of a commission that specified a particular length for the carpet. Fortunately, parts of the inner guard stripe have been preserved along the right-hand edge of the rug (now missing its border), which allows one to be quite sure of the original width of the example. The border, which is of the later "Holbein" type, features a continuous angular Kufic-like interlace.

In general, it can be said that "Holbein" and "Lotto" carpets, which were manufactured during the golden age of Ottoman art, have very little in common stylistically with other forms of decoration from the period. But Amy Briggs, who wrote a comprehensive study about the geometric characteristics of Timurid carpets often depicted in miniature paintings,[13] demonstrates that we have here a classic example of long-lasting design traditions: Timurid patterns continued to be used throughout the height of Ottoman art.

STAR USHAK AND MEDALLION USHAK CARPETS

The concept of coupled decorative motifs arranged in staggered rows provides a link between the Star Ushak and Medallion Ushak carpets, and the "Holbein" and "Lotto" type of carpets discussed above. Their weaving structure as well as their colour schemes are often quite similar, but their designs display strong stylistic differences. The main motifs are far larger in the Star and Medallion Ushak type of rugs so that each individual design segment is proportionately larger, and one could even say that the decorative motif of the Star Ushaks could be described as medallions. The basic Star Ushak motif is always comprised of eight pointed stars of two different types, developing from an essentially square-shaped centre.

In the majority of Medallion Ushaks, the centre features a large ogival medallion, whereas the corners of the field are filled with quarter medallions of a different design and smaller scale. Some of the large-format examples, such as Cat. 7, display repeat patterns of the main motifs, and the smaller medallions can be clearly seen interrupted by the border.

Another important innovation, whose style was anchored in early Ottoman and Timurid carpets, consisted of a network of floral and foliate arabesques on a monochrome ground filling the field in the intervening area of the medallions. This was the fundamental decorative element that Kurt Erdmann termed a "revolution in design".[14] Among the Timurid and early Safavid sources of inspiration of Anatolian carpet weavers was the early Persian north-west medallion carpet design which gave way to the more simplified star version of the Ushak rugs,[15] along with the classic early Safavid medallion with its shield-shaped pendants.[16] At the beginning of the sixteenth century, these Persian decorative motifs were held in high esteem by Ottoman artists, and were featured not only on carpets but also on bookbindings, metalwork and ceramics.

Cat. 6 STAR USHAK
Western Anatolia, circa 1700

Length: 290 cm, width 167 cm

Warp: wool, white, Z2S

Weft: wool, red, Z2, 1st straight, 2nd wavy

Knots: wool, symmetrical, 2Z, V 26–29, H 40

Selvedge: overcast in yellow, braided in the direction of the weft

Ends: not original

Provenance: art market, 1980s

Literature: Jenkins, Keene and Bates 1983, p. 147; Atil 1990, p. 298

Inv. no. LNS 17 R

In this example the repeat pattern is very neatly arranged within the field, wherein the central axis features the only complete representations of the decorative motifs, since the borders cut off more than half of the adjacent medallions and lozenges on all four sides. The two dark blue medallions on either side of the central dark blue lozenge, which marks the centre of the carpet and is the only complete lozenge in the design, are set against a bright brick-red ground filled with floral and foliate motifs in a diagonally angular network of arabesques, distinguishable in practically all examples of the type.

Along the entire border is a very formal band of reciprocal crenellation in blue and red, of a type often seen in Star Ushak carpets, which always contain a somewhat tight scroll of split palmettes. The carpet from the Philadelphia Museum of Art published by Charles Grant Ellis[17] provides a model for Cat. 6, and its details, such as the lively outlines of its two main decorative motifs and the more varied nuances of its colour scheme, show that the rigidity of our example is not due to the design itself. The distinctive stylistic features and the selvedge finish, together with the coarseness of the wool, provide this carpet with some semblance to the so-called "Transylvanian" carpets (see Cat. 13).

Detail, Cat. 6 (LNS 17 R)

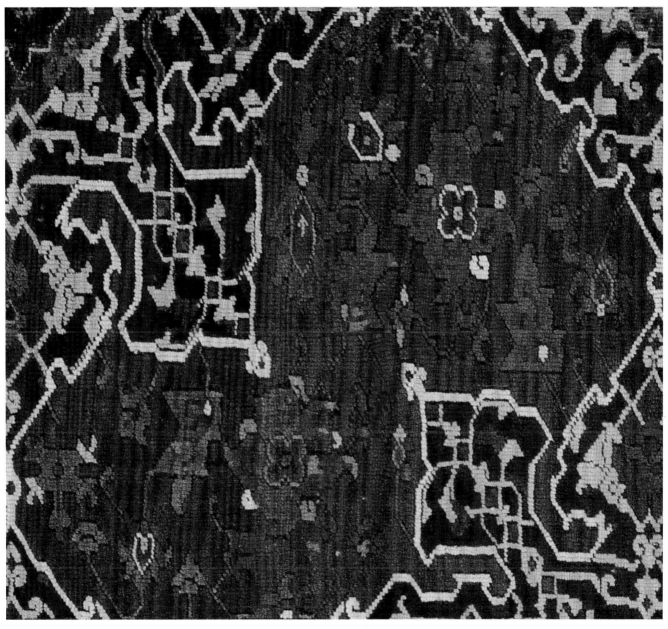

Detail, Cat. 6 (LNS 17 R)

Cat. 7 MEDALLION USHAK
**Western Anatolia,
early 16th century**

Length: 723 cm, width 330 cm
Warp: wool, white, Z2S
Weft: wool, red, Z2, 1st straight, 2nd wavy
Knots: wool, symmetrical, 2–3Z, V 38, H 42
Ends: lower end original, border partly new,
upper end original
Provenance: art market, 1982
Literature: Jenkins, Keene and Bates 1983, p. 146;
Salmon 1984, ill. 16;
Blair and Bloom 1994, fig. 294;
Blair and Bloom 1997, p. 243;
Denny 1999, p. 7;
Klose 2002, p. 61;
Curatola 2010, cat. 116

Inv. no. LNS 26 R

Detail, Cat. 7 (LNS 26 R)

The decorative scheme of most Medallion Ushak carpets is based on two main motifs essentially comprised of a central ogival medallion and peripheral stellated medallions. The latter are generally quartered in each of the four corners and sectioned by the border edges, whereas the ogival medallions are positioned along the long axis of the rug, and are exhibited whole with very small segments of the motif along the border edges. This example illustrates the fact that the design was intended as a repeat pattern, and there is no finer specimen than this unusually large and majestic carpet.

The dominant, red-ground ogival medallion is repeated in two horizontal rows, which alternate with the staggered rows of stellated medallions with light blue grounds, which serve both to accentuate the short central axis and to fill the two narrow ends of the field. The red medallions on this example are typical of early Medallion Ushak rugs, their centres being filled with four-part motifs formed by arabesques of elegant split palmettes. Sixteen-sided stellated medallions of identical form can be seen on countless other carpets, and in early examples such as this they are filled with small, off-white to yellow arabesques of split palmettes and gracefully curling vines issuing floral motifs. Equally graceful arabesques issuing lively yellow flower and leaf decorations fill the dark blue ground, and a characteristic feature of this arabesque is the absence of clear contour lines surrounding the elements of the design. This early Ushak carpet is enlivened by its use of vivid shades of red, yellow and blue, through to the light blue of the stellated medallions.

The border consists of a continuous crenellation, wherein each individual crenel is formed by bifurcated slender palmettes that enclose a lotus blossom on a red ground interspersed with flowers that range from yellow and light blue to green.

This large-format Ushak gives us a good idea of the kind of courtly commissions that were carried out in this region. Furthermore, for two or three centuries this was the most sought-after type of carpet in the castles and palaces of Europe. In England, even as early as the sixteenth century, very successful imitations were already being made that matched the originals in every aspect but the colouring.[18]

Detail, Cat. 7 (LNS 26 R)

MULTIPLE-NICHE CARPETS (SAFF)
AND PRAYER CARPETS

There are no specific instructions in the Qur'an regarding the type of surfaces on which the faithful must perform their prayers. On the other hand, it was related in the liturgies (*tuqus*) and commentaries that at times the Prophet Muhammad performed prayers on his own garment, as well as on a mat woven from palm leaves (*khumra*), and it was recommended that prayers should be performed on clean surfaces, whether mats, reed mats, skins or rugs.

The multiple-niche prayer rugs are decorated with continuous compartmented rows to accommodate large gatherings of worshippers, wherein each compartment serves to define the field in which the worshipper places himself to face the *qibla* or Makkah as instructed by the Qur'an (Chapter 2: verse 150). In a congregational mosque, the rows or *saff* are laid out parallel to the mihrab, or recessed architectural niche in the mosque that indicates the direction towards the *qibla*. The compartments of the *saff* are generally inspired or styled on the mihrab niche, and in many instances are depicted with a mosque lamp pendant from a chain suspended from the apex of the niche, which symbolizes the Chapter of Light from the Qur'an: "Allah is the Light of the heavens and the earth. A likeness of His Light is as a niche and within it a lamp. The lamp is enclosed in glass and the glass is as it were a brilliant star" (Chapter 24: verse 35).

Muslims are called to prayer five times a day, but as they cannot always reach a mosque in time for prayers, they often carry a small-format or single-niche prayer rug or *sijjada* (Turkish *seccade*), allowing them to pray at home, at work or on a journey, and which for practical purposes tended to be light.

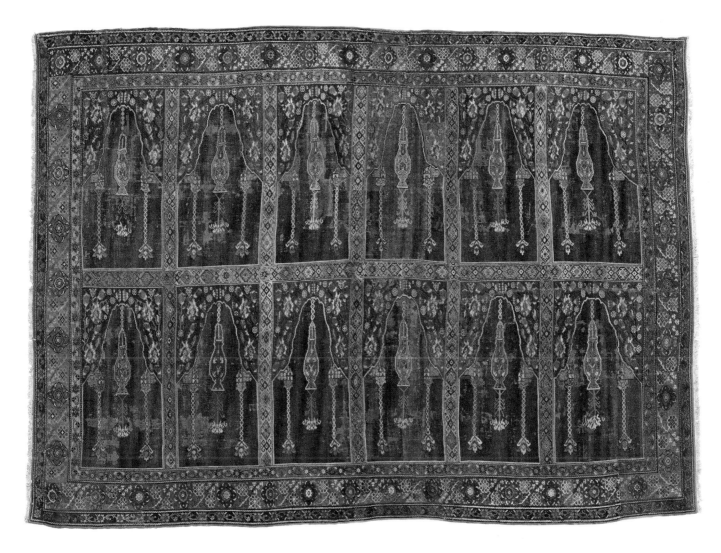

Cat. 8 OTTOMAN MULTIPLE-NICHE PRAYER CARPET
Ushak region, early 18th century

Length: 520 cm, width 360 cm
Warp: wool, white, Z2S
Weft: wool, red, Zx2, 1st straight, 2nd wavy
Knots: wool, symmetrical, 2Z, V 20–22,
H 24–25
Selvedge: 4 warps overcast with wool, green
Provenance: art market, 1980s
Literature: Denny 1999, p. 31

Inv. no. LNS 34 R

It is likely that the world's richest collection of *saff* rugs belongs to the Türk ve Islam Eserleri Müzesi in Istanbul, which inherited numerous examples from Turkish mosques. Quite understandably, European interest in these carpets was very limited before the major carpet exhibitions around the turn of the twentieth century.

The example presented here is comprised of twelve niches arranged in two rows outlined or set apart by running bands of regular pattern motifs. Each niche has an elongated or conical arch of rather awkward shape, and features a mosque lamp suspended from a chain that splits into three smaller chains. The pale-blue body of the lamp is decorated with a stylized flowering plant of late Ottoman style, and a pendant lily stem with three white flowers is suspended from the foot of the lamp. The central axis of the niche is flanked by two "columns", whose load-bearing function would generally be defined by a base and capital, as is the case in earlier examples (such as Cat. 9). However, here the columns do not touch the floor, and instead of having a capital and a base, their ends are decorated with floral motifs.

If we turn our attention to the blue-ground spandrels of the arch, it is noticeable that the floral motif is symmetrically arranged, but that the flowers and vines themselves are non-identical and not evenly distributed. The outlining border of the carpet shares this stylistic feature. Overall, these features not only suggest a lack of focus in the design, but also a widespread production rate in a large workshop of the kind that we can imagine existed in Ushak between the late seventeenth and the nineteenth century. This *saff* was probably not made before 1700, and is likely to date from the early eighteenth century.

Detail, Cat. 8 (LNS 34 R)

Detail, Cat. 8 (LNS 34 R)

Cat. 9 OTTOMAN PRAYER CARPET
Bursa or Istanbul,
2nd half of 16th century

Length: 172 cm, width 125 cm
Warp: silk, yellow and green, Z2S spun
(or S2Z, according to Herrmann
1978–88)
Weft: silk, dark red, 2S, 1st straight, 2nd wavy
Knots: wool and cotton (white and light
blue), asymmetrical, V 84–88, H 92
Selvedge: over 2 green warp bundles
Former
Collection: T. A. Emmet of Amberley Castle,
England;
Eberhart Herrmann, Munich
Provenance: art market, 1982
Literature: Herrmann 1982, vol. IV, no. 1, p. 57;
Jenkins, Keene and Bates 1983, p. 157;
Atil 1987, p. 226; Atil 1990, p. 296

Inv. no. LNS 29 R

When this prayer rug came up for auction at Sotheby's in 1982, there was an unusually intense bidding activity between a number of museums and private collectors. Moreover, it is interesting that European lettering was stitched onto the plain field of the niche and both horizontal cartouches. This element was not consistent with a sixteenth-century Ottoman prayer carpet, and its significance remains unclear, hence the feeling of uncertainty with regards to the dating of the piece, and the connection with the Turkish weaving centre of Hereke famous for its nineteenth-century production, which was quite unjustifiably alluded to as a possible source. The carpet fell into the hands of a London dealer, who "liberated" it from its foreign elements, though, as far as I am aware, he unfortunately kept no record of the activity. Not long afterwards, the carpet reappeared, shining forth from the title page of the catalogue *Seltene Orientteppiche IV*,[19] in which Eberhart Herrmann published the examples displayed in his annual exhibition. The small group of six unusually fine prayer carpets,[20] including three fragments, had been enriched by an additional example.

When one examines carpet designs, one rarely starts with the border. Here, however, the border is rendered with such wonderful attention to detail that it is impossible to resist primarily directing one's attention to it. The pale greenish-blue cotton ground provides the base for one of the most magnificent border designs in Ottoman art, wherein a scroll of eight-petalled rosettes alternates with luxuriant serrated *saz* leaves issuing lotus blossoms, which are always oriented towards the outer edge of the carpet. This motif is augmented by slender vines bearing carnations, white tulips and hyacinths, and red umbel-like flowers creating an overall reciprocal effect. In addition, the vine issues eight-petalled rosettes which flank the principal motif at even distances along the outer edge of the border. The four corners are reflected precisely along a 45-degree angle, in which a white tulip acts as a kind of axis, marking the point at which the horizontal changes to the vertical, and vice versa. Two regular small-pattern edging stripes frame the border. The entire design is masterly.

The plain, wine-red ground of the niche creates the greatest contrast with the border. Its comparative absence of decoration, enlivened by its distinct shimmering colour, provides the ideal basis for concentration required by a worshipper during prayer. The arch of the niche is formed by elegant and well-proportioned lobed spandrels filled with a symmetrical pattern of scrolling floral vines on a white cotton ground. From the apex of the arch hangs a lamp suspended by three chains. The arch itself is supported by two slender columns, whose load-bearing function is clearly indicated by their capitals and prismatic bases which are firmly rooted to the "ground".

Above the niche, the horizontal pair of ochre-ground cartouches contain greenish-blue lotus blossoms halved by the horizontal edging lines, augmented by split palmettes and lotuses in counterchanging orientation, and straddled by a vine bearing six-petalled white flowers.

Detail, Cat. 9 (LNS 29 R)

There can be no doubt that the above-mentioned fine group of seven prayer carpets were all commissions carried out by a court workshop. Furthermore, during the sixteenth century, Bursa was known not only for its outstanding silks and brocades, which were produced in large quantities both for the court in Istanbul and for export to Europe, but also for its carpet workshops, whose production is well documented and whose work was of the same superior quality. The finest Ottoman carpets that are likewise part of the "Bursa" group reflect the style of the sixteenth-century Ottoman court, which is already celebrated for its sophisticated tiles and ceramics produced by the workshops of the neighbouring town of Iznik, and used in the finest buildings of the empire. Manuscripts, bookbindings, and other works of art in leather and semi-precious stones competed with carpets and textiles to attain the most perfect expression of the court's style, and to contribute to the respect and admiration accorded to the sultans.

Detail, Cat. 12 (LNS 24 R)

EARLY VILLAGE RUGS FROM ANATOLIA

It is not by accident that the preceding Ottoman court carpet is followed here by this village variant decorated with motifs of generally the same genre. There could hardly be a better way of illustrating such contrasting types than by presenting them side by side. The court carpet communicates a sense of refinement, detailed naturalism and subdued colours, whereas the village example conveys an impression of vigorous stylized forms rendered in intense colours. The court weavers had to tie more than twice as many knots for the upscale examples, and the use of silk warps gave an impression of continuous flow to the lines, especially when curving shapes were required. The tulips in the village carpets are oriented horizontally, and the large-scale lotus blossoms are repeated ten times, their stylized lines producing an immediate and strong impression on the observer.

Through to the early 1980s, one of the methods used to date classical oriental carpets was founded on the so-called style categories. Within these categories, it was the more or less faultless models that set the standard for carpet workshops. Anything that deviated from this kind of standard was looked upon as a lapse in craftsmanship, and was dismissed as a poor imitation from a later date. This "Westernized" approach was reinforced by an additional restrictive factor: more than three-quarters of the known classical carpets ended up in Europe or elsewhere in the West. Most of them were sent there immediately they were made as merchandise, souvenirs or gifts to European courts, churches, monasteries and wealthy merchants, and were handled with care as "exotic" goods.

These carpets, however, which broadly speaking might be termed goods for export, amounted to just a small proportion of those actually woven in a particular region or at a particular time. For every Eastern household – whether in a village home or a tent – carpets and woven floor coverings were essential utilitarian articles. It is worthy of note that everyday examples and decorative furnishings of the kind produced for the middle classes rarely survived from the era of the classical carpet. They were in common use, and in due course wore out, only to be replaced by newly made versions. Very few of these private masterpieces endured over the following centuries, and if they did, were likely to be shoved unceremoniously into the corners of mosques as charitable donations (*waqf*). It was not until the early 1980s that individual carpets of this type began to attract attention, and a tentative re-evaluation began with regard to their dating.[21]

Until recently, stylistic comparisons had led to unjustifiably late attributions, and hence to a biased assessment of their quality. Village carpets were made on domestic looms, wherein versions evocative of well-known workshop motifs and designs were reproduced with individual variations. These carpets were certainly created during the same period as the workshop carpets, but were stripped of their embellishment; the weavers took pleasure in the resultant clarity of their work, and enriched their unique and individual products with vibrant colours.

Wilhelm von Bode was alone in his eagerness to acquire works of the type for the collection in Berlin, and he alone was responsible for some of these carpets coming to the Museum für Islamische Kunst,[22] where they lay more or less ignored for some eighty years, fortunately managing even to survive the Second World War. It was only when work began on the Berlin museum catalogue that their unique charm and beauty were revealed to the public. In that same year (1988), the catalogue of the Vakıflar Museum in Istanbul was also published.[23] This brought together a representative selection of endangered specimens from mosques from various Turkish regions, to be exhibited in Istanbul, which caused an unprecedented re-evaluation of types among collectors,[24] and created an enthusiastic demand. Sadly, only one such example has found its way into the al-Sabah Collection.

Cat. 10 RUNNER
Central Anatolia, Karapınar/
Konya region, c. 1600

Length: 500 cm, width 112 cm
Warp: wool, white, Z2S
Weft: wool, red, Z2, 1st straight, 2nd wavy
Knots: Z2, symmetrical, V 43, H 27
Provenance: art market 1982
Literature: Eskenazi 1982, pl. 5;
Jenkins, Keene and Bates 1983, p. 149

Inv. no. LNS 21 R

For the most part, the general observations regarding this group of carpets apply to this example with its unusually elongated format. Apart from the above-mentioned tulip motifs and the dominant lotus blossoms within a heavily feathered garland, the palmette trefoil is an added element of decoration often found in village rugs from the Karapınar region.

The long borders are decorated with a festoon bearing closed tulips alternating with red buds oriented towards the outer edge of the carpet. The original upper end-weave band consists of three widely spread palmette trefoils, connected at the corners by skewed palmettes, the execution of which seems to have proved troublesome to the weaver. The same border pattern, which also appears on kilims, is found on several comparable pile carpets that have been carbon-dated from the sixteenth to the seventeenth century.[25]

The yellowish ground is a reliable indication that this piece came from the central Anatolian region of Karapınar/Konya.

Detail, Cat. 10 (LNS 21 R)

Cat. 11 VILLAGE RUNNER
Central Anatolia, Ladik, c. 1800

Length: 434 cm, width 116 cm
Warp: wool, white, Z2S
Weft: wool, red/bright red, Z2,
1st straight, 2nd wavy
Knots: wool, 2Z, symmetrical, V 44, H 30
Selvedge: wool, red, Z, over a bundle of 4 warps
Provenance: art market 1981
Literature: Jenkins, Keene and Bates 1983, p. 148

Inv. no. LNS 19 R

A comparison with the preceding runner reveals some related features on a basic design level. Whereas, for example, the "octagonal" form of the abutted central medallions has been retained, here the filler motif includes a rosette from which radiates a pair of tulips and a variety of flowers. Small tendrils border the sloping sides of the octagonal medallions at regular intervals, and are obviously a development from the flatter feathery motifs that border the central medallions of the previous example (Cat. 10).

A surprising number of carpets based on this pattern have been preserved,[26] but with wide variations in colour and wool quality. This suggests an intensive and relatively long-lasting production that lasted well into the nineteenth century.

Many examples of parallel pattern structures, including ones of the likes of Ghiordes, Ladik, Bergama and Milas carpets, are attested not only in Turkey but also in the Caucasus and Persia. These names embody various themes that enable us to identify places of production during the nineteenth century. Such terms were originally used by dealers to designate the place of purchase but they were gradually incorporated into carpet literature as the century progressed. From the nineteenth century onwards, workshops once again wove large numbers of carpets for export, and these formed the basis of carpet culture in European and American households for more than a hundred years. Additional impetus for the sale of carpets and kilims came from the fashion-setting trade fairs held in Paris (1867), Berlin's Gewerbemuseum (1871) and Vienna (1873).

Late workshop carpets of this type should not be confused with "village rugs", even if they were also woven in villages, that is to say, in village workshops. Generally the same patterns were repeated so frequently that all artistic spontaneity was lost. This work practice also led to the use of synthetic dyes which became increasingly common in the last quarter of the nineteenth century, triggering the decline of Eastern textile dyeing traditions.

Detail, Cat. 11 (LNS 19 R)

Cat. 12 MEDALLION CARPET
Western Anatolia/
Bergama, 18th century

Length: 358 cm, width 194 cm
Warp: wool, white, Z2S,
white-brown in places
Weft: wool, red, Z, 2 shoots
Knots: wool, 2Z, symmetrical, V 31, H 22
Selvedge: wide selvedge over 4 warps in light
blue, red, green, stitched in the
direction of the weft
Ends: wide kilim end (13 cm) in stripes
(red/green/red)
Provenance: art market 1980s
Literature: McMullan 1965, cat. 80

Inv. no. LNS 24 R

Carpets from the transitional period, or between the late classical era and the nineteenth century, are rarely found in Anatolia or Persia. This is a well-known fact, and yet, so far no one has come up with a convincing explanation for the phenomenon. Were there fewer carpets produced at this time, or were there particular reasons why the Western world lost interest in this type of Near Eastern product? One observation might be helpful in this context: the few dozen Anatolian carpets which can be attributed with any certainty to the eighteenth century are of relatively small format. Their length rarely exceeds 380 cm, unless the carpet is an elongated narrow runner. In addition, the halls and rooms of Western palaces and residences were evidently more sparingly stocked with carpets than had been the case a hundred years earlier.

This example,[27] and another closely related to it, displays all the signs of heavy wear known as the "Turkish condition", which emphasizes the assumption that they were not exported to Europe until the twentieth century, and possibly came from mosques that had received them as charitable donations (*waqf*).

Here the pattern is clear and rigorously symmetrical. The central medallion is in the tradition of small-format Ushaks,[28] and is set within an "octagonal" red field which extends vertically in both directions to form a pair of very distinctive niche shapes with broad horizontal crossbeams. The two most recurrent rosette motifs in the field are very similar to the corresponding forms used in the Bergama region.

The border design is of particular interest. Nesting foliate motifs are arranged on a square plan, in which the handling of the colour distribution conveys a pinwheel effect. The repetition of these squares creates a kind of lattice which is somewhat reminiscent of "Lotto" carpet designs. Borders of this type, which are clearly distinct from the more common vine meanders, are evidently characteristic of the post-classical eighteenth century.[29]

Furthermore, later adaptations of this pattern[30] show that the design had become associated with the Bergama region.

"TRANSYLVANIAN" CARPETS

Transylvania, which lies in present-day Romania, was part of the Ottoman Empire from 1526 to 1699.

Emil Schmutzler, who wrote the earliest monograph on these carpets,[31] which had already been singled-out as a group from an early date, gathered numerous interesting sources demonstrating that Transylvania was not only an important trading centre for carpets destined for export to Europe, but that it also imported a great many carpets. In Transylvania they acquired a valued status as church furnishings, an unusual setting for "foreign" goods, but an important factor that allowed them to outlast Turkish rule, as well as the churches in which they were held, despite the upheavals of history.

In 1914, the Museum of Applied Arts in Budapest (Iparmuvészeti Múzeum) held an exhibition of more than a hundred Turkish carpets that had remained in the country,[32] and it was on this occasion that the term "Transylvanian" carpet may have first been coined. In 1922, following the third edition of Bode and Kühnel's publication, the name became firmly established in carpet literature, although not yet clearly defined. About this classification, Kühnel wrote: "The ... next piece is the most common form of the so-called 'Transylvanian' carpet, a label that is inappropriate but nonetheless still popular among dealers and collectors."[33] It might have been expected that the term would subsequently be clarified in Schmutzler's monograph, in which he identifies twelve different groups of Turkish carpets in Transylvania. There initially may have been a tendency to assume that all these examples were "Transylvanian", but it transpires, almost incidentally, that he explicitly only gives the name to the eleventh of the twelve groups.

This group is of the small-format type with borders of angular cartouches, whose centres are filled with paired stylized vegetal motifs arranged in counterchanging orientation, and which, in certain cases, are interspersed with stellated rosettes. The field designs could be divided into two types: one dominated by a pair of vases containing flowering branches symmetrically arranged in relation to the horizontal axis; and another centring on a medallion of concentric lozenges and of rows of flowers.[34] The colour of the ground varies between red, dark blue or a tone of yellow.

A second comprehensive monograph, that covers all design and manufacturing aspects of "Transylvanian" carpets, was written and published in 2005 by Stefano Ionescu,[35] who restricts the term "Transylvanian" to four groups decorated with different patterns. As these are indeed distinct from other contemporary Turkish carpets, the definitions are easy to follow. Ionescu identified the kind of prayer carpet illustrated here (Cat. 13) as "Transylvanian", or of the type in which Turkish design tradition was quite pronounced by comparison to the Ottoman court masterpiece referred to earlier (Cat. 9). The handling and arrangement of stylized floral motifs in Cat. 13 are somehow related to those of the Ottoman court carpet (Cat. 9), but there nevertheless is quite a contrast with the elegance and subtle naturalism of the border on the courtly example. The pale-coloured, unpatterned niche has a sharply pointed arch whose contours appear straggly and off-course, a typical feature of niches of a later period. The light-ground spandrels are decorated with rather rigid, though symmetrical, floral arabesques, while the horizontal band at the top of the field glows with a strongly contrasting blue. The powerful and harmonious colours secure a special place for this carpet in the very extensive – especially in the eighteenth century – and very popular category of prayer carpets. Later examples originate from the western Turkish town of Milas, so it could be speculated that these early "Transylvanian" prayer carpets were also woven there.

Cat. 13 TRANSYLVANIAN PRAYER RUG
17th–18th century

Length: 157 cm, width 112 cm

Warp: wool, yellowish, Z2S

Weft: wool, reddish Z2, 1st straight, 2nd wavy

Knots: wool, 2Z, symmetrical, woven with the niche at the bottom, V 46, H 45

Selvedge: over 3 warps, stitched in the direction of the weft

Ends: 1 cm of red kilim end-weave, 2 cm of yellow kilim end-weave

Provenance: art market 2001

Literature: *Hali* 2001, p. 41 (left); Sotheby's 2001, lot 50

Inv. no. LNS 65 R

Cat. 14 TRANSYLVANIAN CARPET
18th century

Length 152 cm (including kilim ends),
width 119 cm
Warp: wool, S2Z, mixture of red and white
Weft: wool, 2Z, red
Knots: wool, 2Z, V 29, H 28
Selvedge: over 4 warps, light greenish wool
Ends: on both sides, 2 cm red kilim
end-weave, then 3–3.5 cm yellow
kilim end-weave
Former
Collection: F. R. Martin, Vienna
Provenance: art market 2009
Literature: Sotheby's 2009, lot 269

Inv. no. LNS 75 R

The rare and late forms of "Transylvanian" carpets feature fields with red medallions and spandrels in diagonally alternating colours.[36] In this example, the alternating colours are blue and yellow, although the colours of the filler motifs remain identical in both sets of spandrels. The centre of the medallion is marked by a lively floral motif reminiscent of late "Ghiordes" rugs, but as most of this example has been rewoven, it is quite possible that what we see here is a deviation from the original pattern. The yellow and white cartouche border is one of the most common border motifs featured on "Transylvanian" rugs.

LATE PRAYER RUGS AND THEIR RECEPTION IN WESTERN COLLECTIONS

Until the 1970s, Western collectors of oriental carpets were influenced by types featured in publications referring to the collections of their highly regarded predecessors, who had set the standards from the 1920s through to the beginning of the Second World War.

Alongside a few classical carpets, these early collections naturally included many examples of the Milas, Ghiordes, Ladik, Muçur, Kula and Kirshehir prayer rugs, types which were displayed in the Österreichisches Handelsmuseum in Vienna, together with the important classical examples that were renowned in Europe.[37] Initially, the prayer carpet tradition derived from "Transylvanian" carpets and from the few local examples that had survived for three or four centuries.

In the late nineteenth century, when "Orientalism" became fashionable in the interior decoration of various Western salons, these carpets proved extremely popular, since their reverie-provoking quality was deemed to be particularly oriental. Turkmen tent bands and saddle bags, along with Anatolian kilims, introduced a romanticized orientalist trend, and the kilims, which were mainly woven in two identical halves, were often referred to as shawls, and served as curtains framing windows.

Scarcely any other category of oriental carpet had been more subjected to the whims of fashion among collectors than the late Turkish prayer carpet. This is well illustrated by a comparison between two important private collections, both of which were exhibited at the Metropolitan Museum of Art in New York, and for the most part remained there. The James F. Ballard Collection,[38] catalogued in 1923, included twenty-seven examples together with three prayer kilims, which were described as follows: "From Ghiordes and Kula in Western Asia Minor come the prayer rugs which constitute a feature of the Ballard Collection."[39] Equally important was the collection of Joseph V. McMullan,[40] but the lack of prayer rugs in the collection drew the following comment: "The well-known prayer rugs called Ghiordes and Kula find no place in this collection. They deviate markedly from the main stream of Turkish thought in both design and color, and they do not possess the vigorous character and spirit which is in the great tradition of Turkish rug weaving." Consequently, this became the starting point for a new interest in ancient peasant and nomadic rugs.

But nowadays, even a prayer rug of high quality from the traditional group is unlikely to cause a great struggle between bidders, although this situation will, one day, once again undoubtedly change.

Any large-scale production of prayer carpets adheres closely to designs that are typical of their place of origin; therefore their provenance is generally not difficult to identify. The classical model (Cat. 13) introduces this sequence of striking details from five prayer carpets in the al-Sabah Collection.

Of all the surviving examples, the most extensive group must be those woven in the western Anatolian town of Ghiordes. In an early example from this group (see detail of Cat. 15, p. 82), the arch is elegantly curved, and the niche is symmetrical, although rather too densely packed with scrolling vines. Just as exuberant is the rectangular field above the niche, which is filled with counterchanging floral motifs in the bends of a floral garland. The support "columns" of the niche resemble chains of flowers, which are somehow curiously growing out of water pitchers (*ibriq*).

Our second example of Ghiordes prayer carpets probably dates from a century later, when the niche comes to a point (see detail of Cat. 16, p. 83), and its sides are rectilinear, rising in stepped fashion. The very dense pattern filling the niche spandrels and the "cloudbands" that fill the horizontal band at the base of the niche are features shared by the earlier example.

As mentioned above, the numerous examples of prayer carpets from the town of Milas in south-western Turkey can be associated with the "Transylvanian" group. Moreover it has been suggested that Milas is where they first originated. The "double-niche" carpet (Cat. 17 ; see also detail p. 83) likewise belongs in the same stylistic chain of development. Its rather misleading name should perhaps preferably be replaced with that of "medallion carpet". The vibrant colour scheme, as well as the long and even pile, are indications that it was made in the late nineteenth century.

North of Aksaray lies the town of Ladik, where prayer carpets tend to display distinctive horizontal bands, wherein vertical and rigid tulip stems, each bearing a single flower, rise from a crenellation (see detail of Cat. 18, p. 82). It is not clear why the frieze of tulips is sometimes situated above the niche, that is, in the orientation the worshipper takes during prayer, as is the case in this example, and at other times it borders the base of the niche, with the tulips pointing towards the worshipper. The earliest examples are notable for their vibrant colours, similar to those found on central Anatolian peasant carpets, and are often woven with a lustrous variety of wool. There are huge differences in the quality of Ladik carpets, which may account for their difference in age. Carpets from earlier periods feature glowing yellows, lively red niches and rich purples, whereas the colours of the "mass-produced" examples of the late nineteenth century are unattractive, look worn and faded, and the quality of the wool is rough and coarse.

Cat. 15 GHIORDES PRAYER CARPET
18th–19th century

Length: 185 cm, width 129 cm
Warp: wool, white and brown, Z2S
Weft: wool, reddish, Z2x
Knots: symmetrical, wool 2Z, V 40, H 55–56
Substantial sections of the red field
have been rewoven.
Provenance: art market 1970s–80s

Inv. no. LNS 3 R

Cat. 16 GHIORDES PRAYER CARPET
19th century

Length: 156 cm, width 119 cm

Warp: wool, white, Z2S

Weft: wool, red, Z2

Knots: wool and cotton, white, Z, symmetrical, V 40–44, H 62

Selvedge: formed by returning red weft over 4 warps

Provenance: art market 1970s–80s

Inv. no. LNS 6 R

Cat. 17 MILAS "DOUBLE-NICHE CARPET"
Late 19th century

Length: 230 cm, width 167 cm
Warp: wool, red, Z2S
Weft: wool, brownish red, Z1–2,
    2 weft inserts
Knots: wool, 2Z, symmetrical, V 25, H 36
Selvedge: formed by returning weft
Provenance: art market 1970s–80s

Inv. no. LNS 4 R

Cat. 18 LADIK PRAYER CARPET
19th century

Length: 171 cm, width 145 cm
Warp: wool, white and brown, Z2S
Weft: wool, reddish, Z, 1st straight,
2nd wavy
Knots: wool, 2Z, symmetrical, V 35, H 46–50
Provenance: art market 1970s–80s

Inv. no. LNS 9 R

Detail, Cat. 15 (LNS 3 R)

Detail, Cat. 18 (LNS 9 R)

Detail, Cat. 16 (LNS 6 R)

Detail, Cat. 17 (LNS 4 R)

CHAPTER FOUR

PERSIA

There are, as yet, no known examples of Persian carpets from the period ranging between the sensational pre-Islamic and post-Sasanian pile carpet fragments in the al-Sabah Collection (the latest of which have been carbon-dated to the eighth century AD) and the Timurid period (AH 771–913/AD 1370–1507). We do, however, know of around a dozen early Anatolian animal carpets, almost all of which are fragmentary and can be dated to the Seljuq period (AH 431–590/AD 1040–1307), and shortly after. Some of these survived in Tibetan monasteries and have made their way into European and North American collections since the 1990s. It is, however, surprising that among those pieces, which were probably transported along the Silk Road through Iran, none can be definitely said to have originated in Iran. Eberhart Herrmann believes that a fragment in his collection featuring two animal heads originated from Iran or Azerbaijan,[1] but it is difficult to accept this provenance without evidence.

The "Spring of Khosrau" carpet is the stuff of legend. We are told that it once adorned the throne room in the Sasanian metropolis of Ctesiphon,[2] and may have measured up to 600 square metres. It is also said to have been set with precious stones, and that in AD 637 it fell into the hands of the Arab conquerors who divided it up among themselves as booty. Given the report about the gemstones and the carpet's huge dimensions, it is hard to imagine that it was a pile carpet.

There is only one small carpet fragment in the Benaki Museum, Athens, from the Timurid period.[3] However, numerous Timurid carpets depicted in miniatures of the period were studied in detail and published by Amy Briggs as far back as 1940, and then again in 1946.[4] Having said that, in addition to carpets shown as floor covers, an astonishing array of textiles, ranging from tent hangings and bedcovers to garments, were depicted in these paintings. Of course, one cannot assume that all were reliable representations, and indeed it is very likely that the colours reflect the medium used on the paintings rather than those of the original models. A repeat pattern comprised of rows of hexagons alternating with rows of stars, a basic

theme recurrent on this type of carpet, shares close affinities with the small-pattern "Holbein", and is alternately depicted in miniatures on a monochrome ground or on a two-colour chessboard pattern. Equally popular among painters was a small-patterned border that followed the same Kufic border principle as the ones seen on early Ottoman carpets, which, however, differed from the originals in that the artists were always at pains to depict neatly resolved corners and luxuriant colours.

Later stylistic phases included arabesque patterns symmetrically arranged along both axes, forming semicircles, circles, cartouches and ellipses. At times these shapes intersected, creating supplemental compartments that were treated as ancillary motifs and given a different coloured ground and arabesque. Later paintings depicted carpets with medallion motifs over the arabesques, or scrolling vines on a monochrome ground, and which, instead of the severe Kufic-style border, featured continuous elegantly curved scrolls. These basic designs and motifs later served as the models that characterized the Safavid carpets of the sixteenth and seventeenth centuries.

The artist Bihzad painted some of the finest carpet images. He was a member of the Herat School, and in 1522 became the director of the library of Shah Isma'il I (r. AH 907–30/AD 1501–24) in Tabriz. It is therefore conceivable that he would have had a direct influence on the production of court workshops, and it is noteworthy that seventeen years later, work on the Ardabil carpet was completed in Tabriz.

SAFAVID CARPETS: THE WORKSHOPS

Surviving examples of Safavid carpets can be divided very clearly into different groups based on their patterns and technical features, but it is, nevertheless, more complex to attribute them to established centres of pile carpet production. We know with certainty that there were court workshops in the various cities that hosted the Safavid court – Tabriz (from 1502), Qazvin (from 1555) and Isfahan (from 1598) – and that these workshops operated from designs supplied to them by artists.

And, as previously mentioned, one could envisage that the painter Bihzad had an influence on early carpet production from Tabriz. Although we are not aware of any attempts to identify specific locations of carpet production in Qazvin, we do know of other centres such as Kashan and Kirman in southern Iran, and Herat in eastern Iran. The French traveller Jean-Baptiste Tavernier, who visited Isfahan between 1638 and 1643, relates that the town's workshops were located in the Maidan district. His accounts focus mainly on silk carpets brocaded with gold and silver threads, now known as "Polonaise" carpets, although he also mentions woollen carpets.

Kashan was famous for its silk work even earlier than Isfahan. As far back as 1604, the Portuguese chronicler Pedro Teixeira recorded that brocaded silk, as well as velvet, was woven in Kashan. Its fame must have spread as far as Europe, because in 1601 King Sigismund III Wasa of Poland commissioned silk and gold brocaded carpets that bore his coat of arms.

Unfortunately, travellers' accounts are less helpful in determining the provenance of woollen carpets, probably because they were thought to be far less impressive than their silk and gold counterparts. The various descriptions are nevertheless not without interest, and may well have been of use to European collectors and buyers. In 1604, Pedro Teixeira regarded the woollen carpets from Yazd as being the best of all carpets.

The Polish Jesuit Father Thaddaeus Krusinski, who reached Iran at the turn of the eighteenth century, lists the regions of Shirvan and Karabagh, the provinces of Gilan, Kashan, Kirman and Astarabad, the city of Mashhad and the capital Isfahan as having court workshops set up under Shah 'Abbas I (r. AH 995–1038/AD 1587–1629). The place attributions commonly found in the literature on classical oriental carpets – such as for example "north-west Iran" for Tabriz, "south Iran" for Kirman, and "east Iran" for Herat – serve to characterize "types" of carpets rather than the specific location of manufacture. Only further research in the regions, drawing on sources such as municipal archives, workshop records and model designs could provide more precise information.

SAFAVID CARPETS: DATING

A few documents, along with four carpets into which a date was woven, provide us with a basis on which to propose sixteenth- and seventeenth-century dates of manufacture. Among them is the wonderful hunting carpet in the Museo Poldi Pezzoli, Milan,

with its central cartouche naming the designer, Ghiyath al-Din Jami, and the date AH 929 (AD 1522–23) or AH 949 (AD 1542–43), considering that one of the digits in the dating inscription is open to debate;[5] and the famous pair of Ardabil carpets, dated AH 946 (AD 1539–40), made by Maqsud Kashani for the mausoleum of Sheikh Safi.[6] These are followed, after a gap of more than a hundred years, by a vase carpet now in the Sarajevo Museum, made by Ustadh Mu'min ibn Qutb al-Din of Mahan, and dated AH 1067 (AD 1656);[7] and a silk carpet from the mausoleum of Shah 'Abbas II (r. AH 1052–77/AD 1642–66) in Qum, woven by Ni'mat Allah of Jawshaqan, dated AH 1082 (AD 1671).[8] Inscriptions on other extant carpets are of a literary nature.

Contemporary accounts by European travellers[9] include a large number of references that are useful for dating, but it must always be remembered that a good deal of time may have elapsed between the manufacture of the carpet and its sighting. European paintings, which are so important for the dating of early Anatolian carpets, play an insignificant part when it comes to Persian carpet production. The only type of carpet that frequently appears in seventeenth-century Dutch paintings is the vine-scroll carpet, also known as "Herat" carpet.[10]

Carpets are often included in Safavid miniature paintings, but their depictions are rudimentary and therefore of little help. Our datings are based largely on stylistic features, such as the quality of the design and the execution of the details, and on the assumption – perhaps through a perspective that is too European – that a stylistic development can be traced. Subjectivity, therefore, plays a very significant part in date attributions.

SAFAVID CARPETS: PATTERN TYPES

Our sources for identifying pattern types stem from around two thousand examples of classical Persian carpets and fragments which can be categorized as follows: compartment, medallion, multiple-niche prayer carpets, vine-scroll, vase, Polonaise and garden carpets. With the exception of the compartmented and Polonaise types, all these varieties are represented in the al-Sabah Collection. The texts that follow will describe the group-specific features exhibited in individual examples.

The interrelated nature of all these designs is accompanied by a surprising homogeneity of technique; within each group, the spin and ply of the warp and weft yarns, as well as the knot type and count, tend to be almost identical. Similarities can even extend to specific shades of colour, and these are sometimes sufficient to distinguish between different groups.

COMPARTMENT CARPETS

The term "compartment carpet" applies to examples that
have their fields divided into segments of different shapes
and colours, but which are always arranged symmetrically.
Depicted in late Timurid and early Safavid miniatures, these
are the rarest of the very early Safavid carpet designs. One
famous pair is shared between the Metropolitan Museum
of Art in New York and the Musée Historique des Tissus
in Lyons.[11]

Their trellis-like pattern is made up of eight-lobed
rosettes with shield-shaped compartments in the intervening
areas. These are filled with motifs including dragons,
phoenixes, cloudbands and arabesques, all of which are
featured in paintings in Timurid manuscripts. If one were to
date them to the very beginning of the Safavid period, that is,
before 1520, one could say with certainty that they originated
in Tabriz. Bihzad, who apparently enjoyed painting the
segmented, multi-coloured fields of these carpets, includes
such a "compartment carpet" as well as a similarly patterned
baldachin in a miniature dated 1488, depicting Sultan Husayn
Mirza with revellers.[12]

Unfortunately, there are no examples of this very rare
group in the holdings of the al-Sabah Collection.

MEDALLION CARPETS

The most popular Safavid carpet designs centre on a slightly
ogival medallion that determines the space of the field. The
corners of the field are decorated by quarter medallions, or
a similar variation, which touch on the edges of the border.
Moving along the central vertical axis, the medallion is
usually flanked by cartouches and shield-shaped pendants.

This was a guiding design principle during the Timurid
and Safavid periods, and was also used in bookbindings,
textiles, manuscript frontispieces, mosaics, frescoes and more
– in other words, that decorative scheme was ubiquitous
throughout this period. In design workshops, only quarter
medallions – that is, of the type forming corner spandrels
– needed to be rendered by designers, because the whole
motif was just a repetition of this specific quarter. In court
carpets, this particular principle of division was generally
underpinned by an additional design layer that stood out very
clearly from the rest of the design;
and almost without exception, it featured a symmetrical
interlace pattern of vine-scrolls of varying widths and form
that were subordinate to the central medallion. The design
could therefore include up to three overlapping layers, which
in turn could be augmented by various types of flowers.
Furthermore, since the layers of vine-scroll and floral motifs
were interchangeable, the same modular elements could
result in a very wide range of patterns. While retaining the
overall symmetry, this basic principle could then be enriched
with hunting scenes and individual animal motifs, thus
giving rise to the classical hunting or animal carpets of the
Safavid period.

Depictions in paintings show that thrones were usually
positioned over the central medallion which served to
designate the position of the ruler; and owing to the four-part
symmetry of the field, one could say that the pattern served
to emphasize the ruler's distinguished status. Although
these types of carpets are stylistically closely akin to regal
representations in miniatures, they were nevertheless still
used as floor coverings, albeit of a very prestigious kind.

Detail, Cat. 19 (LNS 28 R)

Cat. 19 **NORTH-WEST PERSIAN
MEDALLION CARPET**
**North-west Iran, region of Tabriz,
early 16th century**

Length: 700 cm, width 299 cm
Warp: cotton, white, Z4S
Weft: cotton, white, Z2S, 2x
Knots: wool, Z2, asymmetrical, V 38–40,
   H 43–44
Selvedge: partly original, cotton,
   around 1 warp bundle
Ends: approx. 1 cm kilim end-weave,
   cotton
Former
Collection: 'Atiya Hanim al-Manastirli, Cairo
Provenance: art market 1980s
Literature: Jenkins, Keene and Bates 1983, p. 140

Inv. no. LNS 28 R

This classical north-west Persian medallion carpet displays all the decorative elements characteristic of the type. The main central motif that fills the breadth of the field is formed by two superimposed eight-pointed star medallions in white and yellow, enhanced by the subtle colour difference of their grounds. The "star branches" of the upper medallion are enlivened with light blue lotus blossoms amidst slightly skewed and rigid floral vines, and its centre is occupied by a small, dark blue eight-pointed star that serves as "focal point" of the carpet.

As defined by the stylistic standards of the type, flanking the medallion along the vertical axis are two elongated cartouches, prolonged by medallions filled with small polychrome lotus blossoms amid scrolling vines of reddish colour on a yellow ground. Scrolling over the greenish-blue ground of the field, along the long axis of the carpet, is a symmetrically laid out small-scale arabesque with various peony and lotus blossoms, but, whereas the design is on the whole characteristic of the type, here the four corners, which generally represent segments of the central medallion, are less clearly articulated.

The border is decorated with a broad and imposing reciprocal scroll of split palmettes, in light and dark blue as well as orange on a red ground, and the narrow white-ground inner edging serves as an attractive dividing line between the field and the border.

It is easy to imagine these early, long-format "palace" carpets replicating a garden both indoors and outdoors, with a throne or couch placed exactly over the medallion when used as a royal floor cover. Flanking the carpet would have been another long-format carpet on which the royal guards would have stood, and another for interpreters and scribes. Of the many miniature paintings that depict similar medallion carpets, two in particular are worthy of note.[13]

Cat. 20 FRAGMENT OF A MULTIPLE-NICHE PRAYER RUG
North-west Iran, Tabriz, early 16th century or earlier

Length: 153 cm, width 260 cm

Warp: cotton, white, Z4–6S

Weft: white cotton, and orange or brown wool, Z2, 3 shoots, 1st and 3rd wool, 2nd cotton

Knots: wool, Z2+3, asymmetrical, V 45–52, H 45–50

Former Collection: Indjoudjian, Paris, 1931;
A. Rabenou, Paris, 1939;
Mrs Harry H. Blum, Chicago, 1982;
The Textile Gallery, London, 1982

Provenance: art market 1982

Literature: Wilson 1931, p. 226, no. 529;
Pope 1938–39, pl. 1171;
Jenkins, Keene and Bates 1983, p. 141;
Varichon 1989, pp. 20, 22, 146–47;
Curatola 2010, cat. 239

Inv. no. LNS 27 R

Since it was first displayed in the exhibition "Persian Art" at Burlington House, London, in 1931,[14] this fragment has been much admired and its age and provenance much discussed. The piece was owned by Ayoub Rabenou, and was published as a *saff* comprised of three niches fitted with a surrounding border which had been joined to the fragment at the beginning of the twentieth century. Even though I have never seen the carpet with these border mounts, I assume the work was done in Hereke, which generally produced the very finest work.

It was only when the piece changed hands in 1982, and went to the Textile Gallery in London, that the appendages were finally removed so that it took on its present-day appearance, thus paving the way for comparison with other fragments that may have come from the same carpet, or possibly from a companion piece. In all probability it was once part of a large mosque carpet, and such fragments would have been scarcely distinguishable from one another.

This prayer rug fragment retains a row of three identically decorated niches bordered by a continuous band of slender floral scrolls on a burgundy ground. Each niche is divided into two almost equal parts by a horizontal line, which develops into a projecting lobed element in the centre. The entire breadth of the lower field of each niche is filled with a primary arabesque of lotus blossoms overlaid on a layer of symmetrical scrolling vines issuing smaller flowers of a more restrained nature – a decorative scheme which is typical of vine-scroll carpet designs. The monochrome and undecorated upper halves of the niches contrast with the densely decorated lobed arches or spandrels that link with the spandrels from the adjacent field, forming a continuous reciprocal crenellation pattern, further enhancing the carpet's elegance. In the centre of the plain field is a cloud knot comparable to decorative motifs in Timurid paintings. Its similarity with crowning elements of Chinese *ju-i* sceptres may be coincidental, although in both cases it is probably meant to represent a cloud, but its position in the plain area of the niche where the worshipper's forehead would have touched the carpet suggests that here the motif has meditative connotations.

A related niche is represented in a miniature depicting the Prophet Muhammad kneeling on a prayer rug in a manuscript of the *Mi'rajnama* attributed to circa 1420–40,[15] in which the spandrels of the niche are likewise charged with floral arabesques, and are distinguished from the geometric decoration in the remaining part of the niche. A further reference of multiple-niche rugs is depicted in a miniature from a *Khamsa* of Nizami, dated AH 866/AD 1461, now in the Topkapi Saray Library, Istanbul.[16]

A closely related fragment in the Museum für Islamische Kunst, Berlin, displays three rows of niches – actually two rows and part of a third row. In between the upper and lower rows of niches, which are both filled with scrolling vines, is a row in which the niches exhibit predominantly monochrome fields occupied by twelve-lobed medallions around which orbit twelve small rosettes. In the two lower corners of the niche are relatively large quartered palmettes, likewise evocative of motifs in Timurid miniature painting.[17] Such motifs, generally referred to as cloud collars, can be seen on embroidered robes, and survive on a famous example in the State Kremlin Treasury, Moscow, whose Chinese origin is undisputed.[18] The form of the spandrels with their double layers of scrolling vines echoes the form and decoration of the spandrels of the other niche carpet fragments.

A large multiple-niche carpet fragment in Istanbul[19] which retains three rows and nine niches combines most of the decorative features of the smaller fragments; in addition, its largely preserved upper border provides us with further information about the aspect of the original carpet. Unusual slender swags of dark blue cloudbands outlined in yellow form a reciprocal meander on a ground of dense scrolling vines issuing split palmettes and blossoms which bear a close resemblance to the vines in the spandrels and lower halves of the niches. The artistry of this vegetal arabesque contributes significantly to the overall harmony of the design and aesthetics of the carpet.

Following the restoration work undertaken in 1982 by the Textile Gallery in London, a new picture emerged which gave rise to a connection between the large Istanbul fragment with its wide cloudband upper border, and our fragment (Cat. 20) with its cartouche and rosette lower border. At the time it was published by Pope, the same cartouche and rosette border was used to surround the fragment on all four sides, which may imply that these borders belonged to two or more similar carpets. As one can assume that this fragment was part of a substantial mosque commission, it is therefore plausible that several workshops were active in its production, and created different border designs. At any rate, it is indisputable that the two fragments are contemporaneous.

Notwithstanding its division into niches, this carpet bears a clear affinity with the group of vine-scroll carpets, as well as with the early and rare carpets of the "compartment" type, both as depicted in miniatures and in extant examples. Despite all this, Sarre's suggested attribution to the fifteenth century would seem to require reconsideration.[20] Unfortunately, he did not leave us with any evidence or argument for a Timurid attribution, and it is only natural that we should be somewhat sceptical of such a dating, since it would mean that this piece was the only large-format Timurid carpet to have survived from the period The fragment was also admired by Erdmann and others, who said that "its design and colouring exemplify the best in Persian carpets of the sixteenth century"[21] – but none ever gave it an earlier dating.

The history of this carpet still remains a mystery. Michael Franses suggests that it was among a group of royal gifts that Shah Tahmasp sent to Sultan Sulaiman in 1556,[22] and Pope mentioned such gifts in his Survey of Persian Art,[23] but did not identify them. A connection of this kind cannot of course be ruled out, but there is no firm evidence in favour of this theory, and indeed there are some arguments against it. Foremost, it would imply that the carpet was produced around that time, of which I am extremely doubtful as I cannot imagine that it was produced as late as was suggested. The style and especially the masterly design of the carpet argue for a date at the beginning of the sixteenth century, if not in the mid- or late fifteenth century, which would correspond with the above-mentioned date of the miniature representing the Prophet Muhammad on a prayer carpet. Early Safavid masterpieces of the likes of the compartment carpets in Lyons and in the Metropolitan Museum of Art,[24] and the Chelsea carpet in the Victoria and Albert Museum, London,[25] could sustain attributions to the reign of Shah Isma'il I (r. AH 907–30/AD 1501–24), who handed out commissions for such works of art from his capital Tabriz. However, after 1514 the city was temporarily conquered by his powerful Ottoman neighbours, who carried off to Istanbul a large number of skilled craftsmen. Although Tabriz remained the capital, in the mid-sixteenth century, subsequent to continuous incursions into Iranian territories by the Ottomans, Shah Tahmasp I (r. AH 930–84/AD 1524–76) transferred the capital from Tabriz to Qazvin, and in 1596–97 Shah 'Abbas I transferred it once again, this time to Isfahan.

Early Safavid workshops are associated with Tabriz, and it is assumed that the early medallion carpets, with their ground of scrolling vines, were produced there. The stylistic features of the vine-scroll carpet (Cat. 21) as well as its technical structure suggest that it was also an early piece made in the first Safavid capital.

Detail, Cat. 20 (LNS 27 R)

VINE-SCROLL CARPETS

Safavid medallion carpets are far more common than vine-scroll rugs, notwithstanding, as mentioned earlier, that vine-scrolls of various types constituted a major part of the decoration of medallion carpets. This variety of carpets, with their fields charged with arabesques of scrolling vines, have been associated in carpet literature with Herat, the capital of the Timurid Empire in Khurasan, although the type has also been assigned to Isfahan, the later capital of the Safavids. The arabesques, generally featured on a burgundy ground, are symmetrically arranged along the central axis of the carpet, and tend to be covered with a fantastical array of floral palmettes with serrated petals at the points of intersections of the scrolls. Their borders, which are generally featured on a dark green or dark blue ground, are decorated with meandering vines of varying degrees of complexity.

The rare and impressive large-format vine-scroll carpets are generally ascribed to around the middle of the sixteenth century, and most feature winding cloudbands, and are sometimes enlivened with animals or scenes of animal combat. By contrast, during the seventeenth century production was prolific, and such carpets were produced in a variety of formats; the arabesques lost their liveliness, and the colours of the floral elements were limited to three. As production increased, so did the floral motifs, which in some cases became the exclusive mode of decoration. In addition, cloudbands lost their former vivacity, and lancet leaves were depicted in two colours, a distinguishable feature which contributes to assign the type to this period.

Vine-scroll carpets were frequently exported, more so than any other type of carpet; no other Safavid carpets were as famous or as sought-after in Europe, and they often feature in seventeenth-century Dutch genre paintings.[26] In India they were so popular that copies known as "Indo-Isfahan" carpets were produced, and even today it can be very difficult to distinguish an original from a seventeenth-century Indian copy. However, the difference in the colour scheme is generally regarded as evidence for their provenance.

Detail, Cat. 21 (LNS 7 R)

Cat. 21 VINE-SCROLL CARPET
**East Persia, Herat (?),
late 16th century**

Length: 226 cm, width 152 cm
Warp: silk, white, Z2S
Weft: 1st and 3rd SZ; 2nd cotton 2Z,
very wavy
Knots: wool, 2Z, asymmetrical, V 76, H 72
Selvedge: partly over a reinforced warp
Ends: top and bottom,
each 1 cm cotton kilim
Provenance: art market 1977
Literature: Salmon 1984, p. 176, fig. 18;
Atil 1990, p. 295, no. 105;
Nanji 1996, p. 304

Inv. no. LNS 7 R

The network of orange scrolling vines outlined in brown that
fill the field is laid out in a four-part symmetry on the vertical
and horizontal axes of the rug whose entire decorative scheme
focuses on floral motifs. The scrolling vines issue lotus and
palmette blossoms of three different sizes, which generally
serve to cover the scrolls at the points where they intersect,
as well as a number of smaller blossoms and unobtrusive little
leaves that fill the intervening areas. This is a clear display of
the Safavid love of flowers, which allows the imagination free
rein without the imperative to emulate a particular species of
flowers. Nevertheless, the scrolls depicted here are somewhat
undistinguished, which prompts one to suggest that the
piece may have been produced during the second half of the
sixteenth century.

The dark blue-ground border, however, makes use of
an older compartment-design scheme consisting of lobed
rosettes, shield shapes and cartouches detailed with diminutive
cloudbands, and the two guard stripes are well proportioned
in relation to the main border.

The design and colours of this rug are manifestly well
balanced, and afford one the delightful sense of being in a
fanciful abundantly floral field.

A closely related piece is in the Corcoran Gallery of Art.[27]

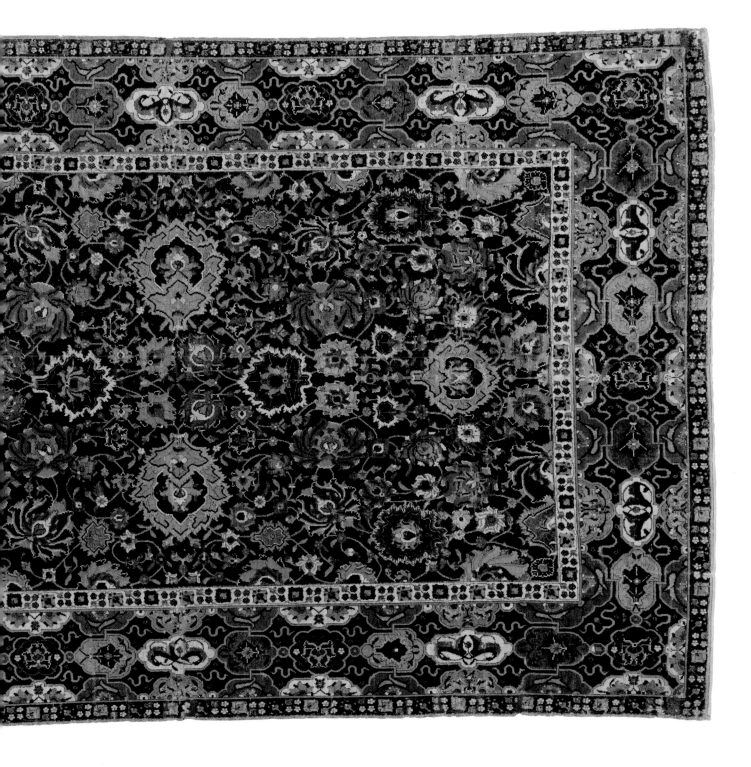

Cat. 22 FRAGMENT OF A LARGE-FORMAT HERAT CARPET
Eastern Persia, Herat, 17th century

Length: 185 cm, width 139 cm
Warp: cotton, white, Z4S
Weft: cotton, white, Z2, 1st and 3rd straight, 2nd cotton, light brown, wavy
Knots: wool, 2Z, asymmetrical, V 46, H 52
Provenance: Gift to the collection

Inv. no. LNS 44 R

This Herat carpet fragment is typical of the type produced and sold to Europe from the early seventeenth century onwards, and it is safe to assume on the basis of the surviving part of the carpet that it once featured a symmetrical pattern of interlacing vine meanders of floral palmettes. Unfortunately, the little that was preserved from the field design only allows us to perceive parts of the dark blue scrolling vines issuing floral palmettes and lancet leaves, and the cloudbands which are interrupted along the edges by the border.

The dark blue ground of the border creates a strong contrast with the deep red ground of the field, and is heightened by the colours of the curved lancet leaves

overturned at their tips, and the elaborate palmette blossoms. The manner in which the corner design was resolved and flawlessly fills the angle of the corner is sufficient to indicate that the carpet was produced in a very good workshop, and probably in Herat.

This variety of vine-scroll carpet was widespread and provided a model for many of the examples woven in India, though the colour schemes varied.

VASE CARPETS

Vase carpets represent a fundamental shift in design by comparison to the types discussed above which centred around a concentric focal point. Here the design plan is replaced by a linear arrangement, which consequently becomes the determining standard whereby everything is laid out symmetrically on either side of a linear progression of flowers. Series of wavy vine lattices that touch on one another form the ogives or lozenge-shaped compartments into which the field is divided. The points where the vines come into contact are generally covered by fanciful flowers, which are always oriented vertically in relation to the design, hence facing the end-weave. The vases that give the type its name obviously face the same direction as the flowers on the vines, and are most often inspired by the shapes of Chinese porcelain vases with a pronounced outward curve at the shoulder tapering down towards a constricted base. Overlapping multi-coloured small-pattern lattices are the most frequent surface decoration on these carpets. A second variant exists in which the ogival lattice is replaced by a similar pattern composed of a network of elongated lozenges with serrated edges that covers the entire field. Their borders are comparatively narrow, and a striking feature is that, in many cases, they have no guard stripes.

Having said that, it is worthy of note that for a carpet to be called a "vase carpet" it does not necessarily have to include vase motifs. In fact, the shared feature of these carpets is an unusual technical structure, in which thick white cotton warps in a "doubled" position are combined with two horizontal brown wool weft shoots and a thin central shoot of silk. These thin silk shoots are not strong enough to hold the thick knots down and generally after long periods of wear they tend to snap, leaving the cotton warps hanging loose in the direction of the warp.

The provenance of vase carpets remains a matter of controversy. From Martin in 1908 through to Erdmann in 1955, it was assumed that they were produced in southern Persia, with Kirman believed to be the production centre. However, Pope did not agree with this attribution. The earliest examples may have been produced around 1600.[28] May Beattie, for whom this group was of special interest,[29] generally attributed them to the first half of the seventeenth century and she considered the vase carpet in the Sarajevo Museum,[30] which is dated AH 1067 (AD 1656), to be an exceptional occurrence.

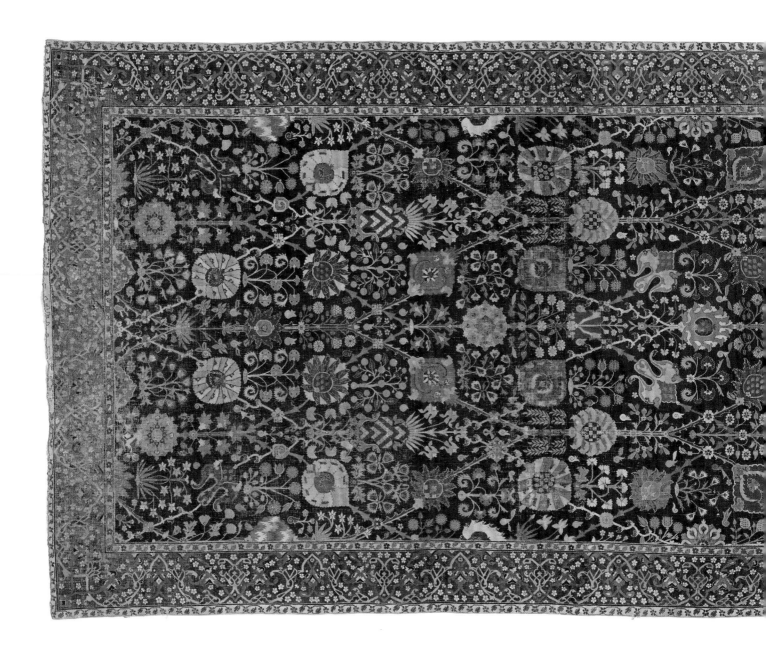

Cat. 23 VASE CARPET
South Persia, Kirman region (?),
mid-17th century

Length: 538 cm, width 208 cm
Warp: cotton, white, Z4S
Weft: cotton, apricot and white, Z2,
very wavy, 2 shoots
Knots: wool, 2Z, asymmetrical,
V 66–68, H 62
Provenance: art market 1982
Literature: Christie's 1982, lot 123;
Jenkins, Keene and Bates 1983, p. 142;
Denny 1999, p. 23

Inv. no. LNS 25 R

This beautiful dark blue-ground vase carpet, with its multitude of coloured blossoms, incorporates two large overlapping serrated vine lattices of gently rounded outline which overlap and form series of small rhomboid compartments. The design is fundamentally planned on three levels, whereby the uppermost plane is taken up by the most prominent and largest lattice pattern, which is made up of two rows of three tangent compartments of pale-coloured vines, two of which are positioned at the centre of the carpet with their tips touching upon the striped vase, roughly placed in the centre of the carpet, whereas the compartments that flank them are interrupted by the border. The second large lattice, which essentially lies on the second plane, is partially covered by the lattice of the uppermost plane and is formed by greenish-blue vines, while the third, and smaller lattice is formed by red and yellow serrated vines.

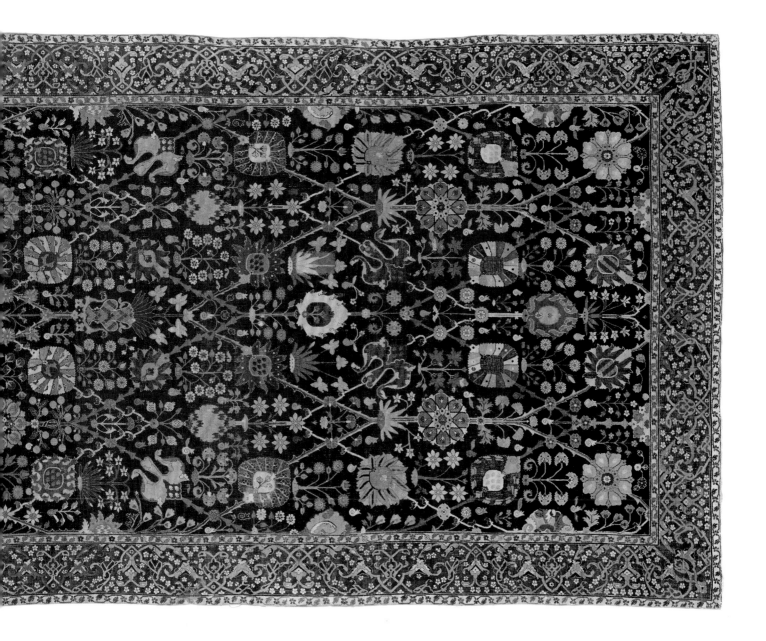

The vines bear a variety of large multicoloured blossoms, which include irises with drooping petals – a relatively rare feature – and which are mostly oriented at an angle, echoing the outlines of the vine lattices. The wide range of small, vertically oriented flower shrubs in the intervening areas, as well as the little white flowers scattered in the border, prompt one to suggest that this carpet was made around the middle of the seventeenth century.

The border is filled with a double reciprocal vine meander of blue and yellow vine scrolls interspersed with small white flowers on a burgundy ground. The pronounced elongated shape of the carpet, more than twice as long as it is wide, which could be characterized as early Safavid, would suggest it was somewhat archaizing.

Cat. 24 VASE CARPET WITH
SHRUB DESIGN
South Persia, Kirman region (?),
2nd half of 17th century

Length: 296 cm, width 183.5 cm
Warp: cotton, white, Z4S
Weft: cotton, brown, Z2S,
1st and 3rd shoots cotton, 2–3Z
Knots: wool, 2–3Z, asymmetrical, V 56–60,
H 45–47
Provenance: art market 1970s–80s
Literature: Denny 1999, text p. 26, fig. p. 22[31]

Inv. no. LNS 5 R

This colourful fragmentary carpet is composed of four large and several small fragments, and exhibits areas of unseemly repair and patching scattered all over the field and borders.[32] The field was joined vertically along the centre, which essentially divides the carpet into two halves, but the borders that run along the longer edges are original to the carpet. The narrow edge borders once belonged to another vase carpet, and were subsequently joined to the field (see Cat. 25). Other fragments of this carpet are known that likewise consist of two joined strips.[33]

The glowing burgundy ground, although worn in most places, still provides an effective backdrop for the yellow, white and blue flowering shrubs. The dark blue-ground borders of the longer edges are filled with reciprocal scrolls that issue slightly angular palmette blossoms and split palmettes in yellow and blue, a colour scheme shared by the appended borders of the narrow edges.

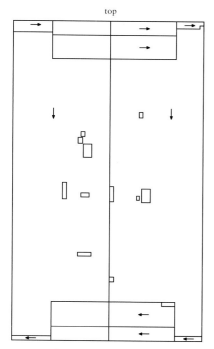

Diagram of Cat. 24 (LNS 5 R), showing direction
of the pile and the actual fragment assemblage

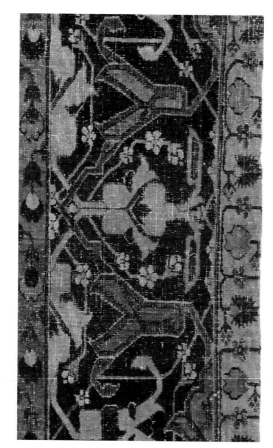

Detail, Cat. 24 (LNS 5 R)

Cat. 25 BORDERS FROM THE
NARROW EDGES OF THE
VASE CARPET WITH SHRUB
DESIGN (Cat. 24)
South Persia, Kirman region (?),
1625–50

Length: 140 cm (?), width 40 cm
Warp: wool, white, Z4S
Weft: 1st and 3rd shoots wool, white, Z2S,
2nd shoot cotton, white, Z2
Knots: wool, 2Z, asymmetrical, V 50, H 61
Selvedge and ends not original

Both dark blue-ground border fragments feature identical pairs of reciprocal palmette scrolls issuing leaves in a lighter blue and yellow, both detailed in red. Fortunately a 2-centimetre-wide strip from the field has been preserved, an indication that the border framed a carpet with a burgundy ground.

A medium-sized fragment of the same border is in Philadelphia,[34] which retains only part of the reciprocal crenellation motif of the inner guard stripe. Another fragment in Berlin[35] includes both guard stripes, as well as a very narrow strip from the field, in which one can distinguish a blue scrolling element, halved red and white rosettes, and a blue tulip. Ellis also illustrates a fragment from the Museum Rietberg, Zurich (acquired in 1962),[36] which may have adjoined the Berlin piece. The rigorous forms and the clear and sensitive colours make this border one of the most magnificent of the whole group of vase carpets.

A fragment that once belonged to Henri d'Allemagne features the same design but with a different colour scheme.[37]

GARDEN CARPETS

Gardens from the Safavid era, or *chahar bagh*s (four gardens), were organized around two main waterways intersecting in cruciform plan, hence roughly creating "four gardens". Parterres of trees and flowers bordered the waterways, and smaller channels interspersed with pools and pavilions at their intersections branched out from the main waterways. Persian rulers delighted in such gardens which were widespread during the reign of Shah 'Abbas I, in Isfahan and Ashraf in the province of Mazandaran.[38]

Figuratively, garden carpets are, so to speak, permanent reflections of these gardens, with the advantage of retaining their beauty independently of the passing seasons. Their design essentially consists of a bird's-eye view of such gardens with their waterways and pools, and the parterres of flower beds and trees that border them. Since gardens were associated with paradisiacal gardens in literature, they transmuted earthly pleasures into the joys of the next world, and were ideally suited places for people to soothe their senses with music and poetry.

The finest and probably earliest example of a Safavid garden carpet is in the Government Central Museum in Jaipur, and was probably a commission or a gift, as a label sewn on its back states that this "foreign" carpet – an indication that it was not woven in India – entered the palace in Jaipur on 29 August 1632.[39] Two other garden carpets can also be confidently attributed to the Safavid period.[40]

The type prevailed in later periods as an independent group of carpets which retained the same basic design features but differed from its Safavid predecessors in the handling of details.[41] The group, which includes the garden carpet (Cat. 26), was produced in north-west Persia during the eighteenth century.

Cat. 26 GARDEN CARPET
North-west Persia, 18th century

Length: 925 cm, width 380 cm
Warp: cotton, white, Z4–10S
Weft: cotton, white, Z4S, 2 shoots
Knots: wool, 2Z, symmetrical, V 25–26, H 44
Ends: lower end-weave: cotton-kilim,
light blue, 5 cm width preserved;
length reduced by horizontal cutting
Former
Collection: Robinson & Co, London 1913;
Lord Aberconway, London;
Wildenstein Collection, New York;
Akram Ojjeh, Paris;
Private collection, Paris
Provenance: art market 1970s–80s
Literature: Conway 1913;
Hawley 1925, pl. VI, p. 160;
Pope 1938–39, pl. 1270, p. 59;
Erdmann 1966, no. 189;
Erdmann 1970, fig. 70;
Klose 1978, p. 113;
Jenkins, Keene and Bates 1983, p. 143;
Varichon 1989, p. 150;
Petruccioli 1994, p. 96;
Clark 1996, p. 41, fig. 34;
Bérinstain 1996, p. 159, pl. 133;
Carboni 1999, p. 101;
Denny 1999, p. 17;
Curatola 2010, cat. 141

Inv. no. LNS 10 R

As mentioned above, the three extant seventeenth-century garden carpets are followed by the group produced in the eighteenth century, and this substantially large carpet from the al-Sabah Collection may well be the oldest of the five or so examples of this later group. It has now been regularly published for almost a century and, at least since it was illustrated by Pope, it has been known as the "Aberconway" carpet.

I shall begin by describing the main waterways that cross the field of the carpet. The rippled surface of the water is rendered in a white and blue stepped chevron pattern, which, in the channel that crosses the central axis of the rug, is oriented from one end of the carpet to the other, whereas in the channel that crosses it the water flow pattern is oriented from the centre towards the outer edges of the rug. Both waterways feed into a square-shaped basin in which stand four peacocks, and where the water surface is rendered in two tones of blue, probably in view of obtaining a darker colour to illustrate the depth of the basin. The two waterways are lined with rows of red and blue cypress trees, in between which are identical red and white flower shrubs on top of which perch pairs of birds.

In addition to serving as divider of the surface, the central waterway also acts as an axis of reflection for the flower beds and smaller channels, which in turn are marked with octagonal "platforms" where their courses cross. These platforms are each decorated with an eight-petalled flower, detailed with a flower in each of its petals. Growing out from each of these platforms, as well as from the main basin, are four oriental plane trees (chinar) with palmate leaves, and a single perching bird. The trees radiate diagonally in four directions from a bird's-eye perspective, and each occupies one of the segments of the carpet (or garden beds). In between the tree-filled segments or "garden beds" are flower beds in which are depicted four lotus blossoms and buds, the only elements that differ slightly from each other in their colour distribution.

Moving towards the upper or shorter end of the "garden" division it is notable that the symmetrical layouts with focal points at the centre of carpets, otherwise common to all classical Persian carpets, have been violated here. This resulted in both octagonal platforms being truncated and the last pairs of birds perching on shrubs being sliced, losing part of their bodies and tails in the process. Hence it would appear that a group of beds has been lost at both ends of the "garden".

A slender scroll issuing red lotus blossoms, buds and leaves runs along the entire white-ground edge, in line with garden-design floral borders.

In short, this garden carpet must have delighted anyone fortunate enough to be seated on it to listen to music and poetry.

Detail, Cat. 26 (LNS 10 R)

THE QUESTION OF INDO-PERSIAN VELVETS

If one were to compare the number of surviving Safavid carpets with the number of surviving Safavid velvets, one would be surprised that, roughly speaking, for every hundred of the former, there is just one of the latter. However, it would be wrong to believe that this is because velvets were subjected to more wear and tear; on the contrary, it can be assumed that they would have been afforded greater care and attention than rugs.

To my knowledge velvets are only mentioned twice in the accounts of European travellers, which are so useful for research in pile carpets, especially with regard to gold and silver brocades.[42] The Chevalier J.-B. Chardin describes the "richesse" of Kashan, and explicitly talks about the "velours" which he saw on his second journey in 1671–73,[43] while Abel Pinçon's account from 1598–99 describes cavalry horses decked in "cloths of brocade on which were represented angels and horses and other animals of all kinds".[44]

Images of angels, such as can be seen on a red-ground velvet with rows of enthroned houris, must have been produced as commissions.[45] Around two-dozen surviving velvets with figural representations provide us with an overview of this extraordinary and wide-ranging art form. Their perfection has often been put on a par with that of miniature paintings, whose themes and motifs they borrowed.[46] But, as already mentioned, motifs such as houris and a portrayal of the Virgin Mary with the Infant Jesus were surely commissioned works – the latter probably for a Christian community in Julfa, the Armenian quarter of Isfahan, where apparently some 40,000 Christians lived during the reign of Shah 'Abbas the Great. Few velvets with large-format centralized motifs match the brightly patterned designs of this special group. Kjeld von Folsach's suggestion that these were decorative panels for the interiors of rooms or tents seems plausible.[47] A very small number of velvets feature a silver or gold ground, and they dispense with figural motifs altogether. As velvets of this type follow the traditions of pile carpet design, we have chosen to end this chapter with these velvets, be they covers or panels.

Until recently, resolving issues related to the attribution of sixteenth- and seventeenth-century velvets to Persian or Indian workshops has more or less been based on style and representation, and we have always been inclined to associate examples featuring large human figures to India even without definite evidence.[48] This method of attribution, although far from being scientific, was mainly based on the intimate relation between the designs of Indian productions with those from the workshops of Isfahan and Kashan.[49] This question continues to be a problem, one that has been debated in carpet literature for at least half a century and remains difficult to agree on.

As this volume was going to press, Elisa Gagliardi-Mangilli studied the velvet in Kuwait (Cat. 27), and proposed an attribution to Indian workshops on the basis of structural analysis. Although an attribution to India was never excluded, if it will soon be possible for scholars to distinguish between Iranian and Indian velvets on the basis of technical peculiarities, one must hope that the matter will finally be set right.

Cat. 27 VELVET WITH SILVER-BROCADE GROUND
Persia, c. 1600, or possibly India, first half 17th century

Length: 180 cm, width 120 cm

Warp: silk, black, burgundy, apricot, green, bright yellow and golden yellow, design with black outline in border

Weft: silver around beige silk core, beige silk

Former Collection: Senator W. A. Clark, Montana 1912, bequeathed to the Corcoran Gallery, Washington in 1926[50]

Provenance: art market 2009

Literature: Riefstahl 1932, no. 2190, pp. 88, 86;[51]
Corcoran Gallery 1948, no. T.3;[52]
Christie's 2009, lot 141

Inv. no. LNS 76 R

Cat. 27 (LNS 76 R) after reconstruction

Only one of the above-mentioned non-figural velvets, but with geometrically laid-out floral medallions,[53] exhibits a field that may have been preserved in its original dimensions. However, even in this case, since the borders have been attached to the field, it does not provide us with a guarantee about the original size of the floor cover, but at least the borders are nicely balanced with the field.

Here the superimposed network of medallions can be reconstructed from the preserved section of the field. The uppermost medallion network outlined in burgundy with a continuous chain of reserved blossoms and buds incorporates short and linear horizontal segments which correspond to conventions known to us, among other sources, from so-called "Polonaise" rugs of the seventeenth century.[54] The second medallion network is outlined in green with reserved çintamani motifs. In between the two interlaced networks runs a delicate pattern of scrolling vines, with beautifully executed floral and foliate motifs that are adequately positioned to fit in the smaller medallions created by the network.

Both networks are each comprised of a complete medallion, and part of a second medallion, although this was evidently intended to be a continuous network, and if just one additional third of the length had been preserved, it would have created the necessary balance clearly suggested by the design. With the inclusion of this lost third, a fourfold repetition of the field would have created a classical symmetry, which would have also been in harmony with the width of the border.[55]

The four corners of the continuous border have been diagonally cut and joined. But since the direction of the warp is identical in the long and short edges of the border, one can assume that it was originally woven as a single continuous strip, which would correspond to two other large-format velvets.[56] The reconstructed version would probably have been 310 × 190 cm.

There can be no doubt that these velvets were produced in court workshops of the type that are known to have existed in Kashan and Isfahan at the time of Shah 'Abbas I. And since these workshops were also commissioned to produce atypical subjects such as "The Virgin Mary with the Infant Jesus", it is not surprising to find foreign Ottoman motifs like the three-dotted çintamani in the green interlaced border. The velvet-woven masterpieces produced in places such as Bursa, where this pattern was part of the standard repertoire, were also highly prized in Persia.

The borders contain a variant of the split-leaf arabesque motif that was used in the early seventeenth century, not only on Polonaise[57] but also on vine-scroll carpets.[58]

A velvet once owned by Stefano Bardini[59] is closely related to our velvet (Cat. 27), although the two designs – a staggered medallion pattern and a double interlace – have little in common. There is general agreement on dating them to around 1600, but there is now a large question mark hanging over the hitherto uncontested attribution to Kashan. The reason for this is the emerald-green interlace with the çintamani motif. All the other motifs are clearly Safavid. This is a recurrence of the issue of pile carpets that bear the contradictory label of "Indo-Persian". Vine-scroll carpet designs that are clearly Safavid were copied in Mughal workshops.[60] Attempts to differentiate them first look at colour nuances: typical Indian colours include a blue-green and a burgundy that blends into pink without any dividing line. However, despite these objections, I am inclined to support a Persian origin.

Cat. 28 VELVET FRAGMENT
Northern India, mid-17th century

Length: 183 cm, width 125 cm
Inner field: length 131 cm, width 70 cm
Border: width 27 cm
Silk velvet
Former
Collection: Comte Odon de Toulouse-Lautrec
Collection, Paris
Provenance: art market 1998
Literature: Drouot 1998, lot 15

Inv. no. LNS 768 T

This relatively small section from what was once a much larger field nevertheless contains all the details necessary for a reconstruction of the design. The central axis features two medallions on a light-coloured ground encircled by pairs of blue bands, around which are entwined vegetal scrolls; one can detect some European influence here. In each of the circular medallions is a flowering plant which appears to have been cut out from a rescued fragment of the velvet and placed on a modern backing. Moreover, the flowering plants which now point in different directions may well have been oriented in the same direction in the original; it is quite likely that the ground consisted entirely of metal brocading, which became so rusty that it simply crumbled.

The rows of halved and quartered blue medallions filling the intervening surface along the edges enclose composite flower shrubs. Interspersed between the medallions in all the rows are small octagons with a central rosette, and in the diagonals between the light and dark-ground medallions is a repeated narcissus flower with a white, five-lobed bloom and blue pinnate leaves, which is a clear manifestation of the Mughal style.

The main emerald-green borders were woven separately and repeat the white narcissus motifs, but here they have wine-red leaves and alternate shrubs of yellow flowers with sword-shaped, wine-red leaves. The pale-coloured guard stripes have been so heavily embroidered that the original floral vine meanders can barely be distinguished.

There are no clues to help us determine the original dimensions of this velvet, but I am fairly sure that it would have been at least four times the size of the surviving fragment.

Detail, Cat. 28 (LNS 768 T)

Detail, Cat. 28 (LNS 768 T)

CHAPTER FIVE
CAUCASUS

DRAGON AND FLORAL CARPETS

In the northern territories of the Safavid Empire lay the Caucasian provinces of Karabagh, Moghan, Shirvan, Daghestan and Georgia, which were administered, on behalf of the Safavids, by the Turkmen chieftain Nadir Quli Khan until he was himself proclaimed Shah and ruled from AH 1148/ AD 1736 to AH 1161/AD 1748. These provinces were finally ceded to Russia in 1813 by the Treaty of Gulistan, while under the rule of Fath 'Ali Shah Qajar (r. AH 1212–50/AD 1797–1834); Russian rule was subsequently extended to Baku, Genje, the Derbent Khanate and the region of Talish.

In 1728 the Polish Jesuit Father Thaddaeus Krusinski wrote that at the beginning of the seventeenth century Shah 'Abbas I had established carpet workshops in Shirvan and Karabagh,[1] consequently, early dragon and flower carpets which are ascribed to this area should therefore be regarded as Safavid. The carpet weavers of the area adopted Safavid field divisions and floral motifs, but reshaped them stylistically to conform to their conventions; hence both the animal motifs and the often large-scale floral motifs are continuations of an archaic and traditional style that is highly distinguishable. This explains why F. R. Martin felt justified in attributing the type from the thirteenth to the fourteenth century.[2] Nonetheless, today it is generally accepted that they were made much later. Moreover, details of Safavid animal carpet designs and the manner in which vase carpets were organized have been acknowledged as forerunners of the type, which precludes any dating earlier than the second half of the seventeenth century.

The "dragon" motifs that give these carpets their name are frequently stylized beyond recognition – to such an extent that it is difficult to classify them as such. The same can be said of the representations of combat scenes of tigers and stags, and of the less common representations of ducks, rabbits and birds. These often unfamiliar animal forms can best be understood by examining the earlier Safavid versions of the design.

The region of Karabagh, in the South Caucasus, is generally accepted as being the source of these carpets, but the question regarding the intended clientele for whom these rather unsophisticated carpets were actually made remains unanswered. This type of rug is most commonly found in mosques of present-day eastern Turkey,[3] and, although it has been suggested, I would completely exclude the idea of exports to Europe or even to southern Persia.

Here for the first time we encounter a problem with wool dyes, in that the large-scale motifs are rendered in such austere tones that the contrast between their assertive forms and dull coloration is hard to reconcile.

Cat. 29 DRAGON CARPET
South Caucasus,
Karabagh region, 18th century

Length: 635 cm, width 247 cm
Warp: wool, white and brown, Z2S
Weft: wool, reddish and brown, 2Z,
1st straight, 2nd wavy
Knots: wool, 2Z, symmetrical, V 37–38,
H 37–38
Ends: the borders have been attached
Provenance: art market 1981
Literature: *Hali* 1979, p. 65; Denny 1999, p. 25

Inv. no. LNS 30 R

One can only speculate on the original length of this carpet, because none of the short end borders are original to the rug. Furthermore, the end which features a row of halved lozenge compartments might have been cut off on account of deterioration. Having said that, it could certainly not have been much longer, as had it been so it would not have corresponded with the conventional proportions of such carpets. The design's progressive orientation is typical of carpets of the type, but the description must be qualified here. The progression or long axis of reflection can be construed as an imaginary dividing line running along the length of the rug, roughly in between the central rows of convoluted dragons. The dragons' heads are recognizable by their elongated snouts, globular eyes, ram-like horns in yellow reserved on the blue ground, and yellow flames that border the blue polygonal compartment, an iconography derived from the Chinese repertoire of the Yuan and Ming periods, as are also the blue cloud ribbons on the dragon's haunches. Humorously, the curled tails of the white dragons terminate in a small trefoil. It should also be noted that the paired dragons depicted along the central axis of the carpet in fact form part of transverse rows of four dragons, in which the remaining two dragons are interrupted by the border, and deformed beyond recognition. Furthermore, the bands that form the essentially lozenge-shaped trellis work feature stylized birds, which are somewhat easier to distinguish than the dragons, and can be identified by their heads, plumage, tails and talons.

In contrast to these inordinately stylized dragon and bird motifs, the appealing and easily recognizable lotuses and palmettes are heartening. One must admit that although associated with the floral motifs, these difficult-to-decipher dragons make us wonder who would have found such representations appealing, and the question remains as to who were the intended owners of carpets such as this.

The characteristically narrow white-ground border decorated with an angular scroll with reciprocal flower motifs in the bends has survived, but the guard stripes on the longer sides of the carpet are missing.

Detail, Cat. 29 (LNS 30 R)

Detail, Cat. 29 (LNS 30 R)

Cat. 30 FLORAL CARPET
South Caucasus,
Karabagh region, 18th century

Length: 472 cm, width 229 cm

Warp: wool, white and brown, Z2S

Weft: wool, light-coloured, 2Z, 1st straight,
2nd very wavy

Knots: wool, 2–4Z, symmetrical, V 34,
H 32–36

Ends: top has been attached

Provenance: art market 1970s–80s

Inv. no. LNS 2 R

Three blue lozenge-shaped medallions mark the vertical axis of this carpet, which is generally consistent with the conventional scheme of the trellis networks in Caucasian dragon carpets. The medallion's blue borders enclose reserved strings of flowers, and their yellow centres are decorated with stylized motifs which could be interpreted as horned bovid heads in frontal view. Each medallion issues four ivory and brown curled lancet leaves.

Between the rows of blue medallions are rows of spiked angular leaves bracketing brown and ivory stylized blossoms among which are blue vertical stems issuing flowers. Touching on the bases of the spiked leaf brackets are small lozenge-shaped medallions enclosing abutted candelabra-like motifs, and which in turn are flanked by fanciful blue foliate motifs.

Most of the pattern is interrupted by the borders of the carpet, but sufficient parts of the various motifs are retained to afford an impression of continuity or flow in the pattern, and the red ground serves both to confine the design and enliven the rather dull colour scheme.

A reciprocal crenellated motif in yellow and dark brown provides a border that comes across as being too detailed and ornate for such a highly patterned field.

Carpets of the type are mainly found in mosques in eastern Anatolia, as is ascertained by a closely related example now at the Vakıflar Museum in Istanbul.[4]

Detail, Cat. 30 (LNS 2 R)

Cat. 31 FLORAL CARPET
     South Caucasus,
     Karabagh region, 18th century

Length: c. 500 cm, width c. 300 cm
        No further details are available,
        as this carpet went missing from the
        collection as a consequence of the Iraqi
        invasion of Kuwait in August 1990
Provenance: art market 1970s–80s

Inv. no. LNS 1 R

The symmetrically laid-out motifs that constitute the design of this carpet include blue-ground medallions amidst a network of bright blossoms, eight-pointed stars and stylized split palmettes, as well as eight-lobed rosettes. All these motifs are common to South Caucasian floral carpets, and are closely related to motifs typically used in eighteenth-century embroideries made in the South Caucasian region of Azerbaijan.[5]

Despite an alleged attempt at symmetry, it is undeniable that the central medallion is closer to the lower border than it should be, and that the eight-pointed star motifs bracketed by split palmettes on either side of the central medallion are not of the same proportion. Furthermore, the brightly coloured halved medallion visible at one end of the rug is completely missing from the other end of the carpet.

As this carpet is now missing it is impossible to comment on its condition, but it appears that the field might have been shortened at one end, and that the narrow edge border was reattached. The lack of clarity in the pattern of the lower corners is a further indication that changes have been made to the carpet.

Detail, Cat. 31 (LNS 1 R)

Cat. 32 KARABAGH RUNNER
South Caucasus, 18th century

Length: 382 cm, width 94 cm
Warp: wool, Z2–4S,
white and brownish
Weft: wool, Z2S, 2x, 1st straight,
2nd wavy, slightly depressed
Knots: wool, 2Z, symmetrical, V 34,
H 28–30
Provenance: art market 1982
Literature: Eskenazi 1982, p. 84, pl. 20

Inv. no. LNS 18 R

In addition to this runner, formerly in the Eskenazi Collection,[6] three more carpets of the type are known to us, two of which are featured on a white ground,[7] one on a dark brown ground,[8] and all four examples have unusually narrow borders.

This carpet is the only example of the type to feature a fourfold repetition of the impressive stylized flower and broad-leaf motif in two-colour variations. In the other three extant examples, only three plant forms are represented. The small space-filling lozenge-shaped medallions and stylized floral motifs that are symmetrically arranged on either side of the dominant motif are clearly derived from the Caucasian flower and dragon carpets motifs described earlier.

This small group is a link between the dragon carpets and the widely produced, almost exclusively small-format carpets, made in various workshops during the nineteenth century. Their diverse range of mostly small-scale motifs can generally be understood as details from larger-format prototypes.

Detail, Cat. 32 (LNS 18 R)

Cat. 33 STAR KAZAK CARPET
South Caucasus,
2nd half of 19th century

Length: 294 cm, width 124 cm
Warp: wool, brown and white flecked, Z3S
Weft: wool, red and brown, 2Z,
symmetrical, V 30–37, H 28
Provenance: art market 1983
Literature: Sotheby's 1983, lot 47

Inv. no. LNS 36 R

Star Kazak rugs are among the most attractive and sought-after nineteenth-century groups of carpets, and although only about twenty extant examples of the type are known, the motifs and colours of Star Kazaks are so striking that it is very easy to understand why they became so popular.

The first monographic feature on these carpets was published in *Hali* in 1980.[9] When publishing his "Orient Stars" collection, Heinrich Kirchheim devoted an extensive treatise to Star Kazaks, and in particular to the origin of their designs.[10] He also stressed the connections between this type and "Caucasian" silk embroideries, which most modern authors now attribute to Azerbaijan.[11] Recent research has added nothing new to these accounts.

Detail, Cat. 33 (LNS 36 R)

Cat. 34 KAZAK PRAYER CARPET
Caucasus, end of 19th century

Length: 144 cm, width 109 cm
Warp: wool, white, Z2S
Weft: wool, red, 2Z, 4-ply
Knots: wool, 2Z, symmetrical, V 26–27, H 29
Selvedge: wool, red, around 2 reinforced warps
Provenance: art market 1970s–80s

Inv. no. LNS 8 R

This prayer rug is distinguished by its clear and straightforward design. The form of its niche is typical of the Kazak region, and very different from the pointed niches one sees on Turkish prayer carpets. Actually, one could say that the top of the arch, with its angled corners, represents a halved octagon. Two lozenge-shaped medallions adorn the centre of the niche, and are flanked by a pair of stylized "tree of life" motifs. It could be conceivable that the two elongated medallions at either end of the row of medallions along the lower end of the field could have pointed to the place for the worshipper to place his feet, while their counterparts above the niche, on either side of the arch, could suggest the placement of the hands during prostration.

The reciprocal border of stepped stylized flowers is typical of nineteenth-century Caucasian production.

CHAPTER SIX

INDIA

MUGHAL CARPETS: PATTERN GROUPS

In view of his Turkic ancestry, one can assume that the Central Asian prince Babur, who claimed descent from the Mongols and Timurids, and who in 1526 founded the Mughal dynasty in India, was familiar with pile rugs. It is also likely that he introduced such carpets to his newly conquered territories before establishing local workshops. By the same token, it is clearly the adoption of Safavid carpet prototypes that makes it so difficult for us to distinguish between the model and later imitations thereof (see, for example, Cat. 21 and Cat. 22), and solutions to this problem are only beginning to be addressed today.

The Mughal emperor Akbar (r. AH 963–1014/AD 1556–1605), grandson of the emperor Babur and great patron of the arts, invited artists and craftsmen from Persia to join his royal ateliers. With his ambition to assemble a library that would make him famous, he did not lag behind his Persian counterparts. He commissioned a fourteen-volume, large-scale manuscript that contained no fewer than 1,400 miniatures painted on cotton, recounting the epic tales of the legendary hero Amir Hamza, uncle of the Prophet Muhammad. This work, known as *Dastan-i Amir Hamza* or *Hamzanama*,[1] was completed circa 1577, and around one hundred of its miniatures have survived the vicissitudes of time. A number of carpets are depicted in these paintings, which belong exclusively to the vine-scroll group (see Cat. 21 and Cat. 22) with borders of reciprocal palmette and lancet-leaf scrolls, including examples with and without central medallions, although none feature animal representations. Until the late sixteenth century, these carpet designs were still unreservedly described as "Persian".

Akbar's court historian Abu 'l-Fazl gives a very factual description of the contemporary Mughal world in the *Akbarnama* and the *A'in-i Akbari*,[2] but carpets and kilims are given only a very brief mention. Although he observes a growth in independent carpet production, with a decline in imports,[3] he mentions that he has seen a large number of Persian carpets and textiles of impressive quality.

The sparse documentary evidence for dating at hand relies mainly on two examples. It is known that in 1630 Robert Bell, a representative of the East India Company, commissioned a carpet in Lahore which he donated to the Girdlers' Company of the City of London in 1634.[4] Five large coats of arms dominate the carpet's narrow field, whose proportions and broad border may be justified by the fact that it was commissioned as a table cover. Here, unfortunately, the subordinate status of the vine-scroll design, together with the proportions dictated by the commission, do not accurately reflect the type of carpets with which Indians chose to surround themselves.

A better idea of carpet production, shortly before the middle of the seventeenth century, can be obtained by way of another carpet, this one commissioned by William Fremlin, whose coat of arms appears several times in the field and border. From 1634 to 1644, Fremlin was in the service of the East India Company in the cities of Ahmedabad, Agra and Surat,[5] hence the carpet was most likely woven in one of these cities before his departure in 1644. The vegetal scrolls and animal representations on this carpet, now in the Victoria and Albert Museum, are rather rigid and not well informed. Furthermore, the technical quality and colour scheme are disappointing, thus making its early date of manufacture rather surprising.

It is now a well-established fact that the cities of Lahore, Agra and Fatehpur Sikri were carpet-producing centres during the emperor Akbar's reign, and that the Girdlers' Company carpet was made in the workshops of Lahore, and that alongside those locations mention was also made of the city of Jaipur.

For the purposes of this catalogue, we have deemed it appropriate to divide Mughal carpets into three main groups: vine-scroll carpets, floral garden carpets and animal carpets.

VINE-SCROLL CARPETS

In the sixteenth century, this type of carpet was the most favoured for representation by Indian miniature painters, and is indistinguishable in its depictions from its Persian counterparts, whereas carpets reproduced in paintings from the seventeenth and eighteenth centuries onward were undoubtedly of Indian design and manufacture. Its distinguishing features did not just lie in the basic elements of design and colour, but in the rendering of details. Depictions of lancet leaves, and naturalistic blossoms of a type that was unknown in Persia,[6] were developed by local workshops, as well as representations of disproportionately large or small lotus blossoms in proportion to the field, alongside the use of graduated colours, such as the blending from a deep red to pink, or a dark blue to light blue.[7]

ANIMAL CARPETS
Regularly depicted in miniature paintings, animal carpets feature hunting or animal combat scenes amidst scrolling vines, which has often led to controversy concerning the early and later phases of Mughal carpet production. A unique set of fragments known as the "grotesque" carpet, astonishing for its surrealism, includes animal torsos in fantastical combinations depicted devouring or disgorging one another. The Musée des Arts Décoratifs, Paris, owns three fragments from yet another carpet in which animal heads are featured almost exclusively as terminals of delicately scrolling vines.[9] The key to these

mysterious fragments remains elusive, and the same is true of another set of fragments that also seem to originate from a single carpet.[10]

Daniel Walker has written a detailed account about this group,[11] and it has been suggested that the mythological *waq-waq* tree could be a clue to interpreting the iconography.[12]

FLORAL GARDEN CARPETS
The fields of this most distinctive group of Mughal carpets are arranged in horizontal rows of flowering plants in repeated variations of floral species oriented in the same direction. The flowers are most naturalistic in appearance – which would have been unthinkable in Safavid carpet designs – and according to Robert Skelton[8] were inspired by European herbals, and began to appear in illuminated miniatures towards the end of the reign of the emperor Jahangir (r. AH 1014–37/AD 1605–27). In a second variant the field is divided into a lattice interlace, where the flowers are featured individually within the lattice's compartments growing from clusters of leaves often depicted curling and overturned. These floral garden carpets display a level of craftsmanship that compares favourably with the very best of Persian production.

Detail, Cat. 35 (LNS 15 R)

Detail, Cat. 35 (LNS 15 R)

Cat. 35 FLORAL GARDEN CARPET
Northern India, 17th century

Length: 508 cm, width 279 cm
Warp: cotton, white, Z4S
Weft: cotton, 1st and 3rd shoots Z2S, white, 2nd shoot S, wine-red, not spun, wavy
Knots: wool, Z2–3, asymmetrical, V 68, H 46–48
Provenance: art market 1970s–80s
Literature: Jenkins, Keene and Bates 1983, p. 144; Brend 1991, p. 224, fig. 159; Denny 1999, p. 24; Curatola 2010, cat. 135

Inv. no. LNS 15 R

Carpet designs laid out in horizontal orientation, as they are on this example, would have been unthinkable in the Persian tradition. No medallions or spandrels interrupt the rows of flowering plants that spread out unhindered in the field, allowing full view of the landscape or garden to unfold before one's eyes; and no architectural elements interrupt the parterre to define the setting, as they do in Persian garden carpets (for example, as in Cat. 26).

A close scrutiny of the naturalistic flowering plants allows us to observe the variety of flowers, which was mainly selected from the *Liliaceae* family, and the botanical accuracy of their rendition. In the lower left-hand corner the horizontal row begins with yellow tiger lilies which, moving right, are followed by martagon lilies, and small five-petalled flowers that are repeated three times in sequence in the lowest row. The next row up starts with a Crown Imperial or *Fritillaria imperialis*, also from the *Liliaceae* family, followed by narcissus, martagon lily and *Lilium grayi*, in this case a series of four flowering plants arranged in a rather staggered row and likewise repeated three times across the field.

Above this row are irises, lilies and roses accurately depicted with toothed leaves and downturned sepals, also arranged in a staggered row. The intervening areas are interspersed with a profusion of small flowering plants and Chinese cloudbands, especially around the upper edge of the field.

In all, the field includes around nine different varieties of flowers rendered in a larger format and a multitude of smaller bunches of flowers, and if one includes the lilium, roses, poppies and narcissi that form the repeat pattern of the blue-ground border, one can truly pronounce this carpet a woven garden. This keen observation of the botanical details of specific flower species was a trend unique to Indian art from the Mughal period.

These fine carpets come from northern India, although it is difficult to determine whether the source was Kashmir or Lahore, and were probably produced in the second half of the seventeenth century.

A comparable piece was auctioned at Sotheby's, London, in 2006.[13]

Cat. 36 FLORAL GARDEN CARPET
Northern India,
end of 17th century

Length: 264 cm, width 192 cm
Reconstructed original length c. 417 cm
Warp: cotton, white, Z4–6S on 2 planes
Weft: 1st and 3rd shoots cotton, brownish,
Z2S, straight, 2nd shoot cotton or
wool, reddish, Z2S, wavy
Knots: wool, 3Z, V 43–46, H 36–37
Composed of several fragments;
see reconstruction
Provenance: art market 1970s–80s
Literature: Varichon 1989, p. 164;
Denny 1999, text p. 22, ill. p. 26[14]

Inv. no. LNS 12 R

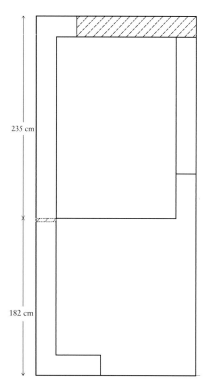

235 cm

182 cm

ABOVE
Diagram illustrating the original size of Cat. 36
(LNS 12 R)

The first impression produced by this example is one of disproportion between the size of the shrubs and the format of the field. But since this is a patchwork – albeit a very successful one – made up of fragments from a single carpet, we have included a diagram illustrating what was once its original size.[15]

We know the original width of the field has been preserved as there are no discernible vertical cuts along the edges; there is, however, a horizontal cut that runs along the lower end of the field, roughly above the second row of shrubs, which is easy to detect at the point where the lower end of the field meets the border. Moreover, the bottom right-hand corner of the main border and inner guard stripe, which have not been tampered with, exhibit skilled handling of "corners"; whereas the lower left-hand corner, which evidently proved problematic when the rug was reassembled, was not executed by taking the treatment or design of the "corners" into consideration. Besides, the pile of the lower border flows horizontally, or in the "wrong" direction, implying it must have once been part of the border of the longer left-hand edge of the rug, whose original length one can therefore estimate to have been 417 cm. To complete the list of cuts, one must also look at the border of the upper edge, three-quarters of which has been joined up to the right-hand corner. The remaining quarter, on the top left, is uncut and includes the end-weave of the long border.

A complete reconstruction of the field would require a borderless fragment measuring around 182 × 126 cm, resulting in the proportions of 1:2.1, which would correspond to the long format of floral garden carpets from the Mughal period.[16]

The surviving section of the field contains seven horizontal rows of flowering plants laid out symmetrically on either side of the central axis, and which are comprised of units of four horizontal rows that are repeated in sequence. Interestingly, a few Chinese cloudbands are scattered between each series of four rows. The bottom row, which has now lost part of the bases of its shrubs includes yellow and blue cup-shaped flowers, red roses and five-petalled flowers; above them are white flowers in what appear to be small vases, and undefined blooms whose petals have yellow edges and blue centres. The floral repertoire is completed by purple irises, poppies and fan-shaped flowers. The original carpet may have well been extended by another repeat of the four basic rows.

The border, with its dark blue ground, is quite solemn in comparison with the fanciful collection of flowering plants in the field. This, I believe, is why Walter Denny spoke of the border as originating from a second carpet, but this hypothesis was probably precipitate.[17] The border gives good grounds to suppose that this carpet was produced at the end of the seventeenth century in northern India, possibly Lahore.

OVERLEAF
Detail, Cat. 36 (LNS 12 R)

Cat. 37 **FRAGMENT OF A
NICHE CARPET**
**Northern India, Kashmir
or Lahore, 1630–40**

Length: 15.6 cm, width 29.7 cm
Warp: silk, white, Z2S
Weft: silk, wine-red, S × 3
Knots: pashmina wool, Z2–4S,
asymmetrical, V 140, H 200
Provenance: art market 1970s–80s
Literature: Sarre and Trenkwald 1926–28, pl. 60;
Walker 1997, fig. 10, p. 25

Inv. no. LNS 16 R

Two equally fine carpets serve as models for the reconstruction of the complete pictorial context of both this fragment, which comes from the top of a prayer carpet, and another from the Benjamin Altman bequest that is now in the Metropolitan Museum of Art, New York.[18] One is the beautiful niche-and-flower carpet from the Thyssen-Bornemisza Collection,[19] and the other is the niche-and-flower carpet from the McMullan Collection, now also in the Metropolitan Museum.[20] The Thyssen-Bornemisza piece features a niche with an apex almost identical to the one depicted on our fragment, which is outlined by two-tone serrated leaves overturned at their tips, and crowned by a two-tone trefoil with serrated petals. A pair of elegantly curved stems terminating in vine leaves seemingly sprout from multi-petalled blossoms, possibly chrysanthemums, which are partially visible on the edges of the fragment.

A paired scroll of serrated orange leaves outlined in red develops from the centre of the border, and meanders in opposite directions along the green-ground border. Abutted S-shape scrolls run along the white-ground stripe of the inner border. Both our fragment (Cat. 37) and the Metropolitan Museum fragment have the same border, indicating that they were once part of the same carpet, as was another piece auctioned in 2004.[21] Sadly, no further fragments of this masterpiece of Mughal carpet weaving have so far come to light.

Cat. 38 **FRAGMENT OF A**
SCROLLING VINES CARPET
Northern India, Kashmir,
c. 1650 or earlier

Length: 45.8 cm, width 26.5 cm
Warp: silk, white, light green and red, Z2S
Weft: silk, wine-red, 2S3, 3-ply,
very depressed
Knots: pashmina, 4–5Z, asymmetrical,
V 106–20, H 100–20
Number
inscribed on
the back: 3852 6 / b0.6
Provenance: art market 1970s–80s

Inv. no. LNS 45 R

Although this fragment is quite small and comprised of several pieces, enough remains to tell us that it comes from one of the most important of all Mughal carpets. Additional fragments from this masterpiece were acquired in 1913 by the Metropolitan Museum of Art, New York,[22] and there is undoubtedly a connection between our fragment (Cat. 38) and the New York fragments. Among the similarities detectable between the fragments are the narcissus flower and white-stemmed leaf outlined in blue that have survived on the right-hand edge of our fragment. Furthermore, both pieces share the same yellow-ground guard stripe filled with a counterchanging scroll of red lilies, which in the case of our fragment has been arbitrarily placed in the lower left-hand corner. The lavish composite blossoms and ribbed stems provide ample proof that the fragments belong together.

Daniel S. Walker dates the New York fragments to around 1650, but the white scrolling cloud ribbons and floral scrolls on the blue-ground border of the Metropolitan Museum fragments are so perfect that I would have no qualms about assigning these fragments to an even earlier date.

Cat. 39 MUGHAL LATTICE
AND FLOWER CARPET
Northern India, Kashmir,
2nd half of 17th century

Length: 664 cm, width 373 cm
Warp: cotton, white, Z6–8S (extremely thin)
Weft: silk, red, Z2S, 1st and 3rd straight,
2nd very wavy
Knots: pashmina, 2Z, V 110, H 100
Provenance: art market 1982
Literature: Christie's 1982, lot 46;
Suckling 2003, p. 102, no. 9

Inv. no. LNS 43 R

Lattice and flower pashmina carpets were very popular in the middle of the seventeenth century and, whereas simple versions exist consisting of regular lattices formed by slender curved leaves,[23] more elaborate versions, such as this example, feature cartouche-like compartments. These compartments, with their lobed and rectilinear segments, are closely related to the decoration on marble architecture from the Mughal period. Furthermore, it is noteworthy that these lattices are generally featured superimposed on a network of vines that issue from the flowers enclosed in the compartments.[24]

The floral motifs in the cartouche compartments of this lattice and flower carpet appear in alternating rows of varied combinations. In the first row, eight small flowers and lancet leaves in a starburst arrangement mark the centre of the cartouche, and are surrounded by pairs of yellow lilies and white chrysanthemums born by foliate spiralling vines in a rhomboid arrangement. In the alternating row of compartments, the centre is marked by a red rose surrounded by pairs of white peonies, and possibly daisies, likewise born by the network of foliate vines. Borders with a dark blue ground are common on carpets of this type, yet here we have a burgundy ground filled with a swagged vine of white and red blossoms that appear to be flanked by mangoes.

The soothing effect of this floral lattice's rhythmic pattern is unfortunately disrupted by the fact that in many places it is in very poor condition. When a carpet of almost 25 square metres has excessively delicate cotton warps and equally fragile silken wefts, it is liable to split and tear. It may well be that the quest for extreme sophistication in the weaving could not stand up to the demands of practical use. However, there is no justification for suggesting that the carpet had been badly handled. No thread can be spun to an unlimited degree of fineness without eventually snapping.

Detail, Cat. 39 (LNS 43 R)

Detail, Cat. 39 (LNS 43 R)

Cat. 40 FRAGMENT OF MUGHAL SILK COMPARTMENT CARPET
India, Deccan, end of 17th century

Length: 192 cm, width 130 cm
Warp: cotton, white, Z9–10S
Weft: cotton, pinkish white, Z5–4, 3 shoots
Knots: silk, Z, asymmetrical, V 51–56, H 56–60
Former Collection: J. Orendi, Vienna
Provenance: art market 1981
Literature: Eskenazi 1982, pl. 35;[25]
Jenkins, Keene and Bates 1983, p. 145;
Walker 1997, cat. 43, p. 148;
Denny 1999, p. 27;
Curatola 2010, cat. 134

Inv. no. LNS 20 R

In Safavid Persia, when weavers wanted to produce a luxury carpet with a high density of knots, silk was the material of choice. Instead, under similar circumstances, Mughal weavers chose pashmina wool. After the middle of the seventeenth century, when silk was chosen as pile material, carpets were generally of medium quality and not of a fine weave.

It is now almost universally agreed that this carpet's place of origin was the Deccan, and most likely Hyderabad.

White slender leaves define the lattice of lozenge-shaped and lobed ogival compartments of this example, and yellow-toothed leaves serve as brackets where the compartments intersect. Typically, the main lattice is overlaid on a slender network of vines issued by the flowering plants enclosed in the compartments. In the lobed ogival compartments are bouquets which probably represent poppies, whereas the lozenge-shaped compartments alternately enclose bouquets of six-petalled flowers and what are probably roses or peonies, in gold and pink.

The burgundy ground of the border is filled with an angular scroll issuing fanciful blossoms and toothed leaves of a different variety than the flowers in the field. The yellow guard stripe, notable for being wider than was customary during that period, is also decorated with an angular scroll issuing pink blossoms.

Up until Daniel Walker's monograph was published,[26] previous literature spoke of a fragment that once belonged to Julius Orendi of Vienna, who published it in his handbook of 1909.[27] That example featured five and a half vertical cartouches framed on three sides by a border. Unfortunately, the quality of the reproduction makes it impossible to distinguish whether the upper border had been joined to the piece, thus making it even longer, or whether it had perhaps already been cut partway along its length.

As far as I am aware, an unpublished fragment in the possession of the heiress to the Alfred Cassirer Collection was exhibited relatively recently at the Museum für Islamische Kunst, Berlin, along with other carpets from the same collection.[28]

Cat. 41 MUGHAL "MILLEFLEURS" CARPET
Northern India, Kashmir, 18th century

Length: 330 cm, width 286 cm
Warp: cotton, white, Z4–5S
Weft: cotton, light blue, 2Z × 2, 1st straight, 2nd wavy
Knots: pashmina, 2–3Z, asymmetrical, V 72, H 72–73
Selvedge: short original segments over reinforced warps
Provenance: art market 1970s–80s

Inv. no. LNS 11 R

The field of this carpet consists of a diagonally laid-out lattice of slender serrated leaves, in which paired rows of blossoms on a yellow ground alternate with a row on a red ground, and one on a blue ground. Filling the lattice compartments are symmetrically arranged rigid bouquets, some of which grow out of tiny vases.

An atypical feature of this carpet is the double border, wherein the border closest to the field is charged with a multitude of flowers in a reciprocal arrangement, and the second border features paired octagons with flowering plants likewise depicted in reciprocal orientation.

The piece is extremely well preserved and belongs to a later group that is dominated by very small floral motifs, which evoke Kashmiri striped textiles, in contrast to earlier carpets with their larger representations of blossoms.[29]

Cat. 42 SUMMER GARDEN CARPET
India, Gujarat (?), 17th century

Length: 330 cm, width 239 cm
Silk chain-stitch embroidery
on white cotton twill weave
Provenance: art market 1998

Inv. no. LNS 50 R

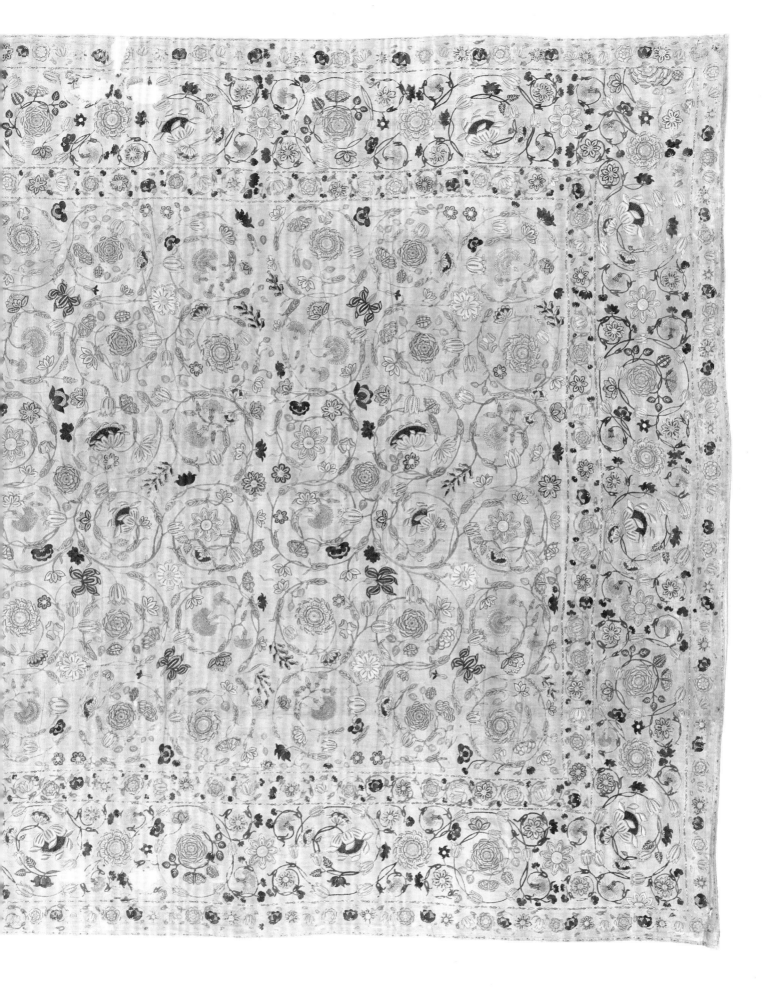

Detail, Cat. 42 (LNS 50 R)

The field of this summer carpet is charged with six horizontal rows of nine spiralling vine scrolls, each of which swirls towards a central blossom, and issues various flowers and leaves in the intervening areas. The upper pair and lower pairs of rows display identical patterns of blossoms, which are repeated, in sequence, three times in each horizontal row.

Accurate botanical representations, once again, enable us to identify roses, carnations, irises and tulips without difficulty, and it is interesting how fine embroidery almost measures up to miniature painting in the depiction of flowers, the precision and accuracy of the rendering bearing witness to the Indian craftsman's keen interest in nature's flora.[30]

The border follows the same decorative scheme as the field, and features pairs of counterchanging scrolls developing from a central blossom with groups of five flowers in beween each pair of scrolls.

Embroidered carpets such as these were sometimes spread on top of woven carpets to lay out objects for presentation,[31] or on marble floors during the summer to provide appropriate seating conditions. They rank among the masterpieces that were the very pinnacle of Mughal luxury.

Cat. 43 SUMMER GARDEN CARPET
India, Gujarat (?),
early 17th century

Length: 387 cm, width 145 cm
Silk embroidery in chain stitch
on quilted white-cotton ground.
Traces of brocading (silver gilt?)

Provenance: art market 1982
Literature: Curatola 2010, cat. 240

Inv. no. LNS 108 T

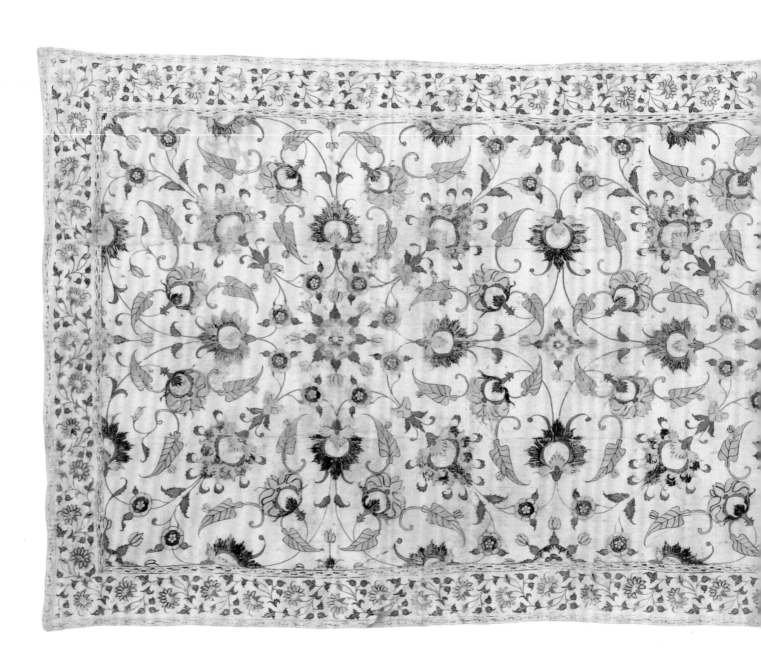

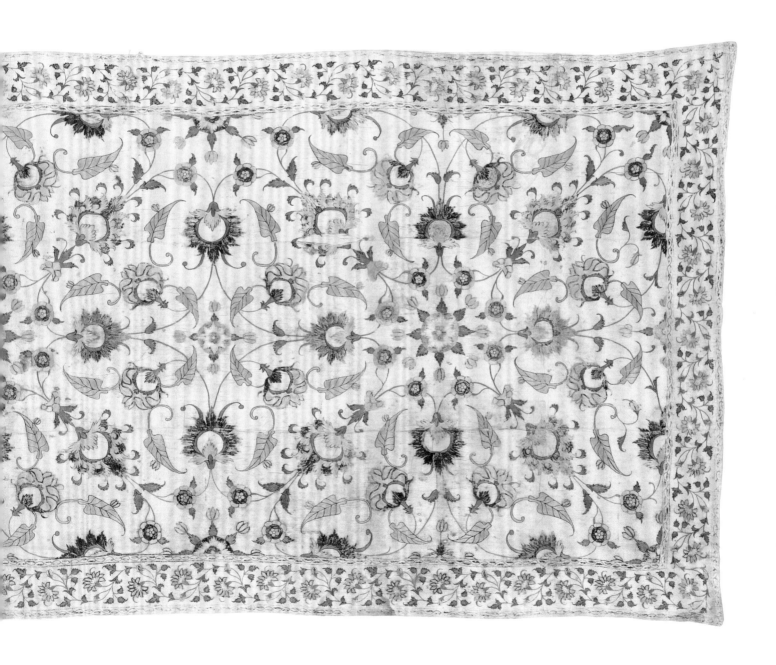

The decorative scheme of this embroidered and quilted summer carpet is closely modelled on the layout of pile carpets. Along the central long axis of the field are three eight-pointed star rosettes, which alternate with rhomboid motifs, dividing the field into three identical sections that centre on the star rosettes. These star rosettes issue red lotus blossoms in four directions, which in turn issue slender vines that form the rhomboid motifs, hence forming an infinite pattern which is repeated horizontally and vertically and a flow interrupted by the border, where the motifs are halved.

Various representations of lotuses and small rosettes as well as two different types of leaves enliven the interstitial areas, and which, thanks to the masterly partitioning of space, do not appear cramped in any way. A pile carpet in the Metropolitan Museum of Art, New York,[32] uses the same field divisions but its pattern appears more congested than the example we have here.

Traces of brocading have been preserved in the centre of one of the flowers, and it may well be that other blossoms were also brocaded as they retain traces of stitching, which wear and especially cleaning may have caused to disappear. As with the preceding summer carpet, we may assume that the carpet originated in Gujarat.[33]

Even without its gilt brocading, this piece of embroidery provides us with a striking example of the original splendour of summer carpets of the type. Once again, the way in which the artists of the Mughal era were able to maintain such stylistic unity and sensitivity remains a source of wonder.

Detail, Cat. 43 (LNS 108 T)

Detail, Cat. 43 (LNS 108 T)

Cat. 44 **MARBLE WEIGHT FOR A**
MUGHAL SUMMER CARPET
India, 18th century

Height: 9.3 cm, width 7 cm
Provenance: art market 1999

Inv. no. LNS 210 S

This small marble carpet weight is carved and inlaid with carnelian, and glass emulating precious stones. Such objects were utilized to weigh down and flatten the corners of light floor coverings, but considerably heavier examples exist that served to weigh down larger and heavier carpets, among which none are known to be inlaid as this example.

The upper end of the weight is carved with an eight-petalled flower, the points of which touch on the lattice pattern which encloses quatrefoils. The octagonal base is decorated with a swagged vine that alternately bears trefoils and leaves, and the same is featured mirrored around the square base.

NOTES

INTRODUCTION
1 Rudenko 1970, pp. 174–75.

CHAPTER ONE
PRE-ISLAMIC AND
EARLY ISLAMIC CARPETS
1 Around forty-one fragments, including two carpets that can be reconstructed, will be presented in a forthcoming volume alongside circa thirty-seven fragments of Sogdian textiles from the late and post-Sasanian periods.
2 Inv. no. LNS 47 R a, datable to AD 240–80.
3 Inv. no. LNS 64 R, datable to AD 130–90.
4 Inv. no. LNS 74 R, datable to AD 265–315.
5 Inv. no. LNS 67 R d and b, datable to AD 310–70.
6 Inv. no. LNS 63 R, datable to AD 300–60.
7 Inv. no. LNS 71 R, datable to AD 500–60.
8 Inv. no. LNS 62 R a, datable to AD 370–470.
9 Inv. no. LNS 1085 T, datable to AD 460–580.
10 Erdmann 1943, p. 36.
11 Spuhler 1988b, p. 54.
12 Gantzhorn 1990, p. 75.
13 Spuhler 1988b, p. 55.
14 Hamilton 1959, pls LXXVI, A and B.
15 Balpınar and Hirsch 1988.
16 Spuhler 1987, p. 69.
17 Spuhler 1968, pp. 102–4.

CHAPTER TWO   EGYPT
1 Erdmann 1938, pp. 179–206.
2 Atil 1981, cat. 14 and 25.
3 Atil 1981, cat. 99.
4 Atil 1981, cat. 4 and 5.
5 Sarre 1923b, pl. II.
6 Erdmann 1938, p. 181.
7 Sarre and Trenkwald 1926–28, vol. I, pl. 46.
8 King and Sylvester 1983, cat. 21 (Palazzo Pitti, Florence).
9 Sarre 1921a, pp. 75–82.
10 de Unger 1980, p. 321.
11 Sarre 1921a; Erdmann 1938.
12 Kalter 1993, p. 74.
13 Achdjian 1949, p. 137.
14 Ellis 1967, fig. 24.
15 Carboni 1999, p. 100.
16 Sotheby's 2000, lot 217.
17 Floret 2004, p. 91.
18 Spuhler 1964, p. 593.
19 Spuhler 1987, cat. 73.
20 Spuhler 1986, p. 264, fig. 4.
21 Balpınar and Hirsch 1988, pls 60 and 61.

CHAPTER THREE   TURKEY
1 The "Holbein" carpet, cat. 5 (LNS 22 R).
2 Martin 1908, vol. 1, p. 113, and vol. 2, pl. 30.
3 Riefstahl and Meyer 1931, pl. 1.
4 Spuhler 1978, cat. 4, pp. 31–32 (text written by the owner).
5 von Folsach 2001, cat. 685.
6 See, for example, Erdmann 1955, fig. 15, "dragon and phoenix" (Museum für Islamische Kunst, Berlin); and fig. 16, the "Marby" rug with confronted birds (Statens Historiska Museet, Stockholm).
7 Kirchheim 1993, pp. 265 ff.
8 von Bode 1902, p. 109.
9 National Gallery, London (The Marriage of the Virgin, inv. no. NG1317); and Hali 1990, pp. 154–55.
10 Kirchheim 1993, p. 15 (now in the Museum for Islamic Art, Doha, Qatar).

11 Unfortunately there are no examples from this group in the al-Sabah Collection.
12 Erdmann 1966, fig. 32.
13 Briggs 1940, figs 27 and 29. See also the Introduction to Safavid carpets (Chapter 4, below).
14 Erdmann 1955, p. 28.
15 Pope 1938–39, pls 1114 and 1112.
16 Pope 1938–39, pl. 1128.
17 Ellis 1988, cat. 23.
18 Spuhler 1964, pp. 593–94.
19 Herrmann 1982, vol. IV, no. 1, p. 57.
20 (a) Museum für Islamische Kunst, Berlin (inv. no. 89,156), published by Erdmann 1955 (1975), fig. 138; (b) Museum für Angewandte Kunst, Vienna (inv. no. T 8327), published by Völker 2001, cat. 6; (c) Metropolitan Museum of Art, New York (acc. no. 22.100.51), published by Dimand and Mailey 1973, pp. 158–59; (d) Museum of Applied Arts (Iparmuvészeti Múzeum), Budapest (acc. no. 15.691), published by Végh and Layer 1925, pl. 20; (e) Türk ve Islam Eserleri Müzesi, Istanbul (no. 775), published by Ellis 1969, fig. 2; (f) Cleveland Museum of Art, Ohio (acc. no. 27.375), published by Ellis 1969, fig. 11.
21 Spuhler 1982, pp. 324–28.
22 See, for example, Spuhler 1987, nos 23, 24, 25, 26, 27.
23 Balpınar and Hirsch 1988.
24 Alexander 1993.
25 Rageth 1999, pl. 9.
26 Brüggemann and Böhmer 1982, cat. 21–22.
27 McMullan 1965, cat. 80.
28 McMullan 1965, cat. 80.
29 Gantzhorn 1990, p. 354.
30 Aslanapa 1987, fig. 154.
31 Schmutzler 1933, pp. 15–16.
32 Csány 1914.
33 von Bode and Kühnel 1922, figs 76 and 77.
34 Schmutzler 1933, pls 46, 47 and 52, 53.
35 Ionescu 2005, p. 58.
36 Ionescu 2005, cat. 133, 146 and 235; Kertesz-Badrus 1985, figs 13 and 61.
37 von Scala and Riegl 1891.
38 Beck and Morris 1923.
39 Beck and Morris 1923, pl. XX.
40 McMullan 1965, p. 295.

CHAPTER FOUR   PERSIA
1 Kirchheim 1993, no. 218, p. 351.
2 Pope 1938–39, pl. 2274.
3 Lentz and Lowry 1989, cat. 119.
4 Briggs 1940, pp. 20–54; and Briggs 1946, pp. 146–58.
5 Pope 1938–39, pl. 1118.
6 Pope 1938–39, pl. 1134.
7 Pope 1938–39, pl. 1238.
8 Pope 1938–39, pl. 1258.
9 On dates of commission and travellers' accounts, see Spuhler 1968, pp. 132–60.
10 Ydema 1991, pp. 59–69.
11 Dimand and Mailey 1973, pp. 134–35.
12 Binyon, Wilkinson and Gray 1933, pl. LXVIII (83a).
13 Robinson 1976, pl. 43, cat. III.201 (1500); and Stchoukine 1954, figs LXXXV and LXXVII (Herat, 1494–95).
14 Pope 1938–39, pl. 1171.
15 Blochet 1926, pl. XXXV: note the apex of the niche. The undated Mi'rajnama manuscript is bound with a Tadhkirat-i Awliya' penned by the same scribe, dated 10 Jumada II, AH 840 (21 December AD 1436). For dating of the manuscript, see Blair 2000, p. 25, and Sims 2002, p. 138, cat. 54.

16 I am grateful to Manuel Keene for communicating to me the reference published by Gray 1979, p. 188, pl. LIX.
17 Stchoukine 1954, pls XLVII and XXXVIII.
18 Pope 1938–39, pl. 1017; Lentz and Lowry 1989, cat. 116.
19 Hali 2007, p. 54.
20 Sarre and Trenkwald 1926–28, vol. II, pl. 50.
21 Varichon 1989, pp. 20, 22, 146–47.
22 Erdmann 1970, p. 157.
23 Pope 1938–39, vol. III, pp. 2334–35.
24 Dimand and Mailey 1973, cat. 6, fig. 67.
25 Pope 1938–39, pls 1131–35.
26 Ydema 1991.
27 Walker 1997, fig. 63.
28 Spuhler 1987, no. 86.
29 Beattie 1976.
30 Pope 1938–39, pl. 1238.
31 In the publication the figure was wrongly substituted with that of cat. 36 (LNS 12 R).
32 See fig. 54, diagram showing the fragment assemblage.
33 Spuhler 1987, pl. 90, p. 88, cat. 25
34 Ellis 1988, pl. 56, p. 200.
35 Spuhler 1987, no. 90, p. 230 (taken from Sarre 1908).
36 Ellis 1988, fig. 56.
37 d'Allemagne 1911, after p. 98 (colour plate).
38 Sarre 1921b.
39 Dimand 1940.
40 Beattie 1976, pl. I (the Wagner carpet) and Völker 2001, no. 93 (the Figdor garden carpet).
41 Spuhler 1987, no. 91.
42 Spuhler 1968, pp. 132–60.
43 Spuhler 1968, p. 132, source 2.
44 Spuhler 1968, p. 149, no. 59 (horse blankets).
45 Pope 1938–39, pl. 1018.
46 Quoted from Pope 1938–39: see pls 1021 (Laila and Majnun), 1038 (Khosrau and Shirin), 1024 (Alexander's Fight with the Dragon), plus genre scenes, pls 1060, 1022 A, 1023 n, 1025 (hunting), 1060 (a wine-drinker), 1059 (a falconer), and 1062 and 1063A (garden scenes). See also Spuhler 1978, nos 92–100.
47 von Folsach 2001, p. 362.
48 Spuhler 1978, cat. 107 and 108, both reportedly from the Palace of Jaipur; and Von Folsach 2001, cat. 663 and 665.
49 The two Polonaise carpets in The Metropolitan Museum of Art, Dimand and Mailey 1973, fig. 87.
50 Christie's 2009, lot 141.
51 Riefstahl lists it as a "Velvet Carpet" and ascribes it to "Turkey, Late XVI Century" (the 1928 edition lists it as a "Polonaise").
52 Where it was listed as a textile, and attributed to late sixteenth-century Turkey.
53 Welch 1987, no. 122.
54 Welch 1987, p. 113, no. 84; Spuhler 1968, p. 271, system XI.
55 See fig. 63 showing the reconstruction of the floor cover.
56 Pope 1938–39, pls 1068 and 1020.
57 Spuhler 1968, p. 280, no. 7b.
58 Pope 1938–39, pl. 1186.
59 Farnham 2001, p. 83.
60 Spuhler 1987, p. 107.

CHAPTER FIVE   CAUCASUS
1 Spuhler 1968, p. 141.
2 Martin 1908, p. 118, note 251.

3 Yetkin 1978.
4 Balpınar and Hirsch 1988, pl. 78;
  Yetkin 1978, pl. 43.
5 Kirchheim 1993, ills 42–56.
6 Eskenazi 1982, p. 84, pl. 20.
7 Völker 2001, no. 122; Kirchheim 1993,
  no. 61, p. 126.
8 Spuhler 1988b, pl. 36.
9 Bausback and Dall'Oglio 1980, pp. 17–26.
10 Kirchheim 1993, pp. 31–81.
11 Kirchheim 1993, p. 78.

CHAPTER SIX INDIA
1 Glück 1925, p. 146; Egger 1974 and 1982.
2 Skelton 1982, cat. 27–32.
3 Phillott 1977, p. 57.
4 Andrews 1905–6b, pp. 1–2; Irwin 1962.
5 Walker 1997, fig. 49, p. 56.

6 Walker 1997, figs 41, 43, 44, 62.
7 Walker 1997, figs 45, 46.
8 Skelton 1972, p. 147.
9 Roux 1977, no. 685.
10 Erdmann 1966, no. 238.
11 Walker 1997, pp. 33–37.
12 Schulz 1914, vol. 1, pl. D (centre).
13 *Hali* 2006, p. 105.
14 The publication figure was wrongly substituted
  with that of cat. 24 (LNS 5 R).
15 See fig. 73.
16 Denny 1999, p. 22.
17 Denny 1999, p. 22.
18 Sarre and Trenkwald 1926–28, pl. 60.
19 Spuhler 1998, cat. 45, the Aynard carpet.
20 McMullan 1965, no. 7, p. 42.
21 *Hali* 2004, p. 102. This fragment of the upper
  border includes the same curving stem that

sprouts from behind the chrysanthemum and
flows towards the trefoil as cat. 37.
22 Walker 1997, figs 78–79.
23 Walker 1997, cat. 29.
24 Walker 1997, cat. 30, 31; Spuhler 1978, no. 60.
25 The text (p. 49) describes seven fragments from
  this carpet or a companion piece, see Thompson
  2004, no. 17, p. 70.
26 Walker 1997, fig. 143, p. 148.
27 Neugebauer and Orendi 1909, fig. 14, p. 25.
28 No catalogue was issued.
29 Walker 1997, fig. 124; McMullan 1965,
  nos 30, 33, 34.
30 Skelton 1982, p. 67, fig. 6a (cat. 62).
31 Skelton 1982, p. 59, fig. 2 and p. 62, fig. 3.
32 Walker 1997, p. 84.
33 Irwin and Hall 1973, pl. 20–21; Ekhtiar, Soucek,
  Canby and Haidar 2011, cat. 266.

BIBLIOGRAPHY

Achdjian 1949
Albert Achdjian. *A Fundamental Art: The Rug.*
Paris, 1949.

Alexander 1993
Christopher Alexander. *A Foreshadowing of 21st
Century Art: The Color and Geometry of Very
Early Turkish Carpets.* New York and Oxford, 1993.

d'Allemagne 1911
Henry-René d'Allemagne. *Du Khorassan au pays des
Bachtiaris: trois mois de voyage en Perse.* Paris, 1911.

Andrews 1905–6a
Fred H. Andrews. *One Hundred Carpet Designs
from Various Parts of India.* London, 1905–6.

Andrews 1905–6b
Fred H. Andrews. "Indian Carpets and Rugs."
Journal of Indian Art 12 (1905–6).

Aslanapa 1987
Oktay Aslanapa. *Türk Hali Sanati'nin Bin Yili.*
Istanbul, 1987.

Atil 1981
Esin Atil. *Renaissance of Islam: Art of the
Mamluks.* Washington, DC, 1981.

Atil 1987
Esin Atil. *The Age of Süleyman the Magnificent.*
Washington, DC, 1987.

Atil 1990
Esin Atil (ed.). *Islamic Art and Patronage:
Treasures from Kuwait.* New York, 1990.

Balpınar and Hirsch 1988
Belkis Balpınar and Udo Hirsch. *Carpets of the
Vakiflar Museum Istanbul.* Wesel, 1988.

Batári 1981
Ferenc Batári. *Regi török sçönyegek Kecskeméten, or
Old Turkish Rugs in Kecskemet.* Kecskemet, 1981.

Bausback and Dall'Oglio 1980
Peter Bausback, Marino Dall'Oglio et al.
"Star-kazaks/Sternkasaks." *Hali* 3/1 (1980).

Beattie 1976
May H. Beattie. *Carpets of Central Persia:
With Special Reference to Rugs of Kirman.*
Sheffield, 1976.

Beck and Morris 1923
J. Beck and Frances Morris. *The James F. Ballard
Collection of Oriental Rugs.* New York, 1923.

Bérinstain et al. 1996
Valerie Bérinstain et al. *L'Art du tapis dans le
monde.* Paris, 1996.

Binyon, Wilkinson and Gray 1933
Laurence Binyon, J. V. S. Wilkinson and Basil Gray.
Persian Miniature Painting. London, 1933.

Blair 2000
Sheila Blair. "Color and Gold: The Decorated
Papers Used in Manuscripts in Later Islamic
Times." *Muqarnas* 17 (2000).

Blair and Bloom 1994
Sheila Blair and Jonathan Bloom. *The Art and
Architecture of Islam 1250–1800.* London, 1994.

Blair and Bloom 1997
Sheila Blair and Jonathan Bloom. *Islamic Arts.*
London, 1997.

Blochet 1926
Edgar Blochet. *Les enluminures des manuscrits
orientaux – turcs, arabes, persans – de la
Bibliothèque nationale.* Paris, 1926.

von Bode 1902
Wilhelm von Bode. *Vorderasiatische
Knüpfteppiche aus älterer Zeit.* Leipzig, 1902.

von Bode and Kühnel 1914 and 1922
Wilhelm von Bode and Ernst Kühnel.
Vorderasiatische Knüpfteppiche aus älterer Zeit.
Leipzig, 1914 (2nd revised edition) and Leipzig,
1922 (3rd revised and expanded edition).

Brend 1991
Barbara Brend. *Islamic Art.* London, 1991.

Briggs 1940
Amy Briggs. "Timurid Carpets: 1.
Geometric Carpets." *Ars Islamica* 7 (1940).

Briggs 1946
Amy Briggs. "Timurid Carpets: 2. Arabesque
and Flower Carpets." *Ars Islamica* 11–12 (1946).

Brüggemann and Böhmer 1982
Werner Brüggemann and Harald Böhmer. *Teppiche
der Bauern und Nomaden in Anatolien.* Munich,
1982.

Carboni 1999
Stefano Carboni. "Reflections of an Ideal World."
Hali 105 (1999).

Christie's 1982
Fine Eastern Textiles Rugs and Carpets,
London, 14 October 1982.

Christie's 1996
The Bernheimer Family Collection of Carpets,
London, 14 Feburary 1996.

Christie's 2009
Art of the Islamic and Indian Worlds,
London, 6 October 2009.

Clark 1996
Emma Clark. *Underneath which Rivers Flow: The
Symbolism of the Islamic Garden.* London, 1996.

Conway 1913
Sir William Martin Conway. "A Persian Garden
Carpet." *Burlington Magazine* 23/122 (1913).

Corcoran Gallery 1948
The Corcoran Gallery of Art Bulletin 2/1 (1948).

Csány 1914
Karoly Csány, Sandor Csermely and Karoly Layer.
Erdélyi török szönyegek kiallitásának.
Budapest, 1914.

Curatola 2010
Giovanni Curatola with Manuel Keene and Salam
Kaoukji. *al-Fann: arte della civiltà islamica:
la Collezione al-Sabah, Kuwait.* Milan, 2010.

Denny 1999
Walter B. Denny. *Zarabi: Carpets: Reflections
of an Ideal World.* Kuwait, 1999.

Dimand 1940
Maurice S. Dimand. "A Persian Garden Carpet
in the Jaipur Museum." *Ars Islamica* 7 (1940).

Dimand and Mailey 1973
Maurice S. Dimand and Jean Mailey. *Oriental
Rugs in the Metropolitan Museum of Art, with
a Chapter and Catalogue of Rugs of China and
Chinese Turkestan.* New York, 1973.

Drouot 1998
François de Ricqlès. *Art d'Orient,*
Paris, 25 September 1998.

Egger 1974 and 1982
Gerhard Egger. *Hamza-nama. Vollständige
Wiedergabe der bekannten Blätter der Handschrift
aus den Beständen aller erreichbaren Sammlungen: 1.
Band: Die Blätter aus dem Museum für angewandte
Kunst in Wien, Graz, 1974 und 2. Band: Die Blätter
aus dem V&A London. II.* Graz, 1982.

Ekhtiar, Soucek, Canby and Haidar 2011
Maryam D, Ekhtiar, Priscilla P. Soucek, Sheika R.
Canby and Navina Najat Haidar (ed). *Masterpieces
from the Department of Islamic Art in the
Metropolitan Museum of Art.* New York, 2011.

Ellis 1967
Charles Grant Ellis. "Mysteries of the Misplaced
Mamluks." *Textile Museum Journal* 2/2 (1967).

Ellis 1969
Charles Grant Ellis. "The Ottoman Prayer Rugs."
Textile Museum Journal 2/4 (1969).

Ellis 1988
Charles Grant Ellis. *Oriental Carpets
in the Philadelphia Museum of Art.*
Philadelphia and London, 1988.

Erdmann 1938
Kurt Erdmann. "Kairener Teppiche, Teil l.
Europäische und islamische Quellen des 15.–18.
Jahrhunderts." *Ars Islamica* 5 (1938).

Erdmann 1943
Kurt Erdmann. *Die Kunst Irans zur Zeit der
Sasaniden.* Leipzig, 1943.

Erdmann 1955 and 1975
Kurt Erdmann. *Der orientalische Knüpfteppich.
Versuch einer Darstellung seiner Geschichte.*
Tübingen, 1955 and Tübingen, 1975 (4th edition).

Erdmann 1962
Kurt Erdmann. *Europa und der Orientteppich.*
Berlin and Mainz, 1962.

Erdmann 1966
Kurt Erdmann. *Siebenhundert Jahre Orientteppich.
Zu seiner Geschichte und Erforschung.*
Hanna Erdmann (ed.). Herford, 1966.

Erdmann 1970
Kurt Erdmann. *Seven Hundred Years of Oriental
Carpets.* Hanna Erdmann (ed.), May H. Beattie and
Hildegard Herzog (trans). London, 1970.

Eskenazi 1982
J. J. Eskenazi. *Il tappeto orientale dal 15 al 18
secolo.* Milan, 1982.

von Falke 1930
O. von Falke. *Die Sammlung Dr Albert Figdor,
Wien,* vol. I. Vienna and Berlin, 1930.

Farnham 2001
Thomas J. Farnham, "Classical Carpets
and America." *Hali* 119 (2001).

Floret 2004
Elisabeth Floret. "Early Aubusson Pile Carpets."
Hali 132 (2004).

von Folsach 2001
Kjeld von Folsach. *Art from the World of Islam
in the David Collection.* Copenhagen, 2001.

Gantzhorn 1990
Volkmar Gantzhorn. *Der christlich orientalische
Teppich. Eine Darstellung der ikonographischen
und ikonologischen Entwicklung von den
Anfängen bis zum 18. Jahrhundert.* Cologne, 1990.

Glück 1925
Heinrich Glück. *Die indischen Miniaturen des
Haemzae-Romanes im Österreichischen Museum
für Kunst und Industrie in Wien und in anderen
Sammlungen.* Zurich, 1925.

Gray 1979
Basil Gray (ed.). *The Arts of the Book
in Central Asia, 14th–16th Centuries.* Paris and
London, 1979.

Hali 1979
Hali 2/1 (Spring 1979).

Hali 1990
"An Early Animal Rug at the Metropolitan
Museum." *Hali* 53 (1990).

Hali 2001
"Turkish Bounty at SNY." *Hali* 119 (2001).

Hali 2004
"Auction Price Guide." *Hali* 135 (2004).

Hali 2006
"Auction Price Guide." *Hali* 149 (2006).

Hali 2007
"ICOC XI: Istanbul – Preview: Exhibitions."
Hali 150 (2007).

Hamilton 1959
R. W. Hamilton. *Khirbat al Mafjar: An Arabian
Mansion in the Jordan Valley.* Oxford, 1959.

Hawley 1925
Walter A. Hawley. *Oriental Rugs, Antique and Modern*. London, 1925.

Herrmann 1978–88
Eberhart Herrmann. *Seltene Orientteppiche* (10 vols). Munich, 1978–88.

Ionescu 2005
Stefano Ionescu. *Die osmanischen Teppiche in Siebenbürgen*. Rome, 2005.

Irwin 1962
John Irwin. *The Girdlers Carpet*. London, 1962.

Irwin and Hall 1973
John Irwin and Margaret Hall. *Indian Embroideries: Historic Textiles of India at the Calico Museum, Vol II*. Ahmedabad, 1973.

Jenkins, Keene and Bates 1983
Marilyn Jenkins, Manuel Keene and Michael Bates. *Islamic Art in the Kuwait National Museum: The al-Sabah Collection*. London, 1983.

Kalter 1993
J. Kalter et al. *Die Gärten des Islam*. Stuttgart and London, 1993.

Kertesz-Badrus 1985
A. Kertesz-Badrus. *Türkische Teppiche in Siebenbürgen*. Bucharest, 1985.

King and Sylvester 1983
Donald King and David Sylvester. *The Eastern Carpet in the Western World from the 15th to the 17th Century*. London, 1983.

Kirchheim 1993
E. H. Kirchheim et al. *Orient Stars: A Carpet Collection*. Stuttgart, 1993.

Klose 1978
Christine Klose. "Betrachtungen zu nordwestpersischen Gartenteppichen des 18. Jahrhunderts." *Hali* 1/2 (1978).

Klose 2002
Christine Klose. "The Turkish Forked-Leaf Border." *Hali* 123 (2002).

Lentz and Lowry 1989
Thomas W. Lentz and Glenn D. Lowry. *Timur and the Princely Vision: Persian Art and Culture in the Fifteenth Century*. Los Angeles, 1989.

Martin 1908
Fredrik Robert Martin. *A History of Oriental Carpets before 1800*. Vienna, 1908.

McMullan 1965
Joseph V. McMullan. *Islamic Carpets*. New York, 1965.

Nanji 1996
Azim Nanji (ed.). *The Arts of Islam*. Detroit, 1996.

Neugebauer and Orendi 1909
Rudolf Neugebauer and Julius Orendi. *Handbuch der orientalischen Teppichkunde*. Leipzig 1909–30 (14 editions).

Petruccioli 1994
Attilio Petruccioli. *Giardino Islamico: Archittetura, Natura, Paesaggio*. Milan, 1994.

Phillott 1977
D. C. Phillott (ed.). *The Ain-i Akbari by Abu'l-Fazl Allami*. H Blockmann (trans). New Delhi, 1977.

Pope 1938–39
Arthur U. Pope (ed.) with Phyllis Ackermann. *A Survey of Persian Art from Prehistoric Times to the Present* (6 vols). London and New York, 1938–39.

Rageth 1999
Jürg Rageth (ed.). *Anatolian Kilims and Radiocarbon Dating*. Riehen, 1999.

Riefstahl 1932
Rudolf Riefstahl. *An Illustrated Handbook of the W. A. Clark Collection*. Washington, DC, 1932.

Riefstahl and Meyer 1931
Rudolf Riefstahl and R. Meyer. "Primitive Rugs of the 'Konya' Type in the Mosque of Beyshehir." *The Art Bulletin* 13/2 (1931).

Robinson 1976
B. W. Robinson (ed.). *Islamic Painting in the Keir Collection*. London, 1976.

Roux 1977
Jean-Paul Roux et al. *L'Islam dans les collections nationales*. Paris, 1977.

Rudenko 1970
S. J. Rudenko. *Frozen Tombs of Siberia: The Pazyryk Burials of Iron Age Horsemen*. M. W. Thompson (trans.). London, 1970.

Salmon 1984
Vanessa Clewes Salmon et al. "The Al-Sabah Collection of the Kuwait National Museum." *Hali* 6/2 (1984).

Sarre 1908
Friedrich Sarre. *Altorientalische Teppiche*. Leipzig, 1908.

Sarre 1921a
Friedrich Sarre. "Die ägyptische Herkunft der sogenannten Damaskus-Teppiche." *Zeitschrift für bildende Kunst*, NF 32 (1921).

Sarre 1921b
Friedrich Sarre. "Ein neuerworbener Gartenteppich." *Berliner Museen* 42/5 and 6 (1921).

Sarre 1923a
Friedrich Sarre. *Die Kunst des alten Persiens*. Berlin, 1923.

Sarre 1923b
Friedrich Sarre. *Buchkunst des Orients*. Berlin, 1923.

Sarre and Trenkwald 1926–28
Friedrich Sarre and H. Trenkwald. *Alt-Orientalische Teppiche* (2 vols). Vienna, 1926–28.

von Scala and Riegl 1891
A. von Scala and A. Riegl. *Katalog der Ausstellung orientalischer Teppiche im K. K. Österreichischen Handelsmuseum*. Vienna, 1891.

Schmutzler 1933
Emil Schmutzler. *Altorientalische Teppiche in Siebenbürgen*. Leipzig, 1933.

Schulz 1914
P. W. Schulz. *Die persisch-islamische Miniaturmalerei. Ein Beitrag zur Kunstgeschichte Irans* (2 vols). Leipzig, 1914.

Sims 2002
Eleanor Sims with Boris Marshak and Ernst Grube. *Peerless Images: Persian Painting and its Source*. New Haven and London, 2002.

Skelton 1972
Robert Skelton. "A Decorative Motif in Mughal Art." In *Aspects of Indian Art*. P. Pal (ed.). Leiden, 1972.

Skelton 1982
Robert Skelton et al. *The Indian Heritage: Court Life and Arts under Mughal Rule*. London, 1982.

Sotheby's 1983
Islamic Works of Art, Carpets and Textiles, London, 20 April 1983.

Sotheby's 2000
Fine Oriental and European Carpets; Including Property from the Collection of Aram K. Jerrebian, New York, 27 April 2000.

Sotheby's 2001
Fine Oriental and European Carpets, New York, 14 December 2001.

Sotheby's 2009
Arts of the Islamic World, London, 7 October 2009.

Spuhler 1964
Friedrich Spuhler. "Eine Ausstellung orientalischer Teppiche in Temple Newsam House, Leeds." *Weltkunst* 34/15 (1964).

Spuhler 1968
Friedrich Spuhler. *Seidene Repräsentationsteppiche der mittleren bis späten Safawidenzeit. Die sogenannten Polenteppiche*. Berlin, 1968.

Spuhler 1978
Friedrich Spuhler. *Islamic Carpets and Textiles in the Keir Collection*. George Digby and Cornelia Wingfield Digby (trans). London, 1978.

Spuhler 1982
Friedrich Spuhler. "Unbequeme Fragen zu unbekannten türkischen Teppichen der Berliner Sammlung" ("Uncomfortable Questions about Unknown Turkish Carpets in the Berlin Collection"). *Hali* 4/4 (1982).

Spuhler 1986
Friedrich Spuhler. "Chessboard Rugs." In *Oriental Carpet and Textile Studies, II: Carpets of the Mediterranean Countries 1400–1600*. London, 1986.

Spuhler 1987
Friedrich Spuhler. *Die Orientteppiche im Museum für Islamische Kunst, Berlin*. Munich, 1987.

Spuhler 1988a
Friedrich Spuhler. *Oriental Carpets in the Museum of Islamic Art, Berlin*. Robert Pinner (trans.). London, 1988.

Spuhler 1988b
Friedrich Spuhler. "Carpets and Textiles." In *Islamic Art in the Keir Collection*. London, 1988.

Spuhler 1998
Friedrich Spuhler. *The Thyssen-Bornemisza Collection: Carpets and Textiles*. London, 1998.

Stchoukine 1954
Ivan Stchoukine. *Les peintures des manuscrits timurides*. Paris, 1954.

Suckling 2003
Katie Suckling. "Review: 'Pure Theatre'." *Hali* 130 (2003).

Thompson 2004
Jon Thompson. *Silk: 13th to 18th Centuries: Treasures from the Museum of Islamic Art, Qatar*. Doha and London, 2004.

de Unger 1980
Edmund de Unger. "The Origin of the Mamluk Carpet Design." *Hali* 2/4 (1980).

Varichon 1989
Anne Varichon et al. *Tapis: présent de l'Orient à l'Occident*. Paris, 1989.

Végh and Layer 1925
Gyula Végh and Károly Layer. *Tapis turcs provenant des églises et collections de Transylvanie*. Paris, 1925.

Völker 2001
A. Völker. *Die orientalischen Knüpfteppiche im Österreichischen Museum für angewandte Kunst*. Vienna, 2001.

Walker 1997
Daniel Walker. *Flowers Underfoot: Indian Carpets of the Mughal Era*. New York, 1997.

Welch 1987
Stuart C. Welch. *The Islamic World*. New York, 1997.

Wilson 1931
Arnold Talbot Wilson. *Catalogue of the International Exhibition of Persian Art*. London, 1931.

Ydema 1991
Onno Ydema. *Carpets and their Datings in Netherlandish Paintings, 1540–1700*. Woodbridge, 1991.

Yetkin 1978
Serare Yetkin. *Early Caucasian Carpets in Turkey* (2 vols). Arlette Mellaarts and Alan Mellaarts (trans). London, 1978.

TABLE OF CONCORDANCE OF INVENTORY NUMBERS
AND CATALOGUE NUMBERS

Page numbers in *italic* refer to pages on which illustrations appear.

KEY TO TECHNICAL ANALYSIS

S-spin:	ply in anti-clockwise direction
Z-spin:	ply in clockwise direction
V:	number of knots per 10 cm in vertical direction
H:	number of knots per 10 cm in horizontal direction
Z2S:	two Z-spun strands plied together in anti-clockwise direction (S)
Z2:	two Z-spun strands with no discernible ply
Asymmetrical:	asymmetrical or "Persian" knot
Symmetrical:	symmetrical or "Turkish" knot

The number of knots per 10 cm (V and H) can be used to calculate the number of warps and wefts. To calculate the knot density per dm², multiply V × H.

INDEX